EXCEL FOR WINDOWS:

THE POCKET REFERENCE

Jeff Woodward

Osborne **McGraw-Hill**

Berkeley New York St. Louis San Francisco
Auckland Bogotá Hamburg London Madrid
Mexico City Milan Montreal New Delhi Panama City
Paris São Paulo Singapore Sydney
Tokyo Toronto

Osborne **McGraw-Hill**
2600 Tenth Street
Berkeley, California 94710
U.S.A.

For information on translations or book distributors outside of the U.S.A.,
please write to Osborne **McGraw-Hill** at the above address.

Excel for Windows: The Pocket Reference

1234567890 DOC 9987654

ISBN 0-07-882009-X

CONTENTS

Acknowledgments

A great deal of work by many dedicated and talented individuals has gone into this book. Unfortunately, I don't know all of these hard-working people, but I want to extend my heartfelt thanks for all the time and effort that they expended on this project.

- Special thanks go to Scott Rogers, who gave me the opportunity to write this book for Osborne McGraw-Hill. His positive attitude and cheerful demeanor were greatly appreciated, especially after he called to see how I was surviving my fifth all-nighter.

- I am grateful to Sherith Pankratz for her efforts early on to point me in the right direction on this project. She was always pleasantly quick to respond to all my requests for assistance.

- I'd like to thank Emily Rader, my developmental editor, for being there every step of the way, keeping me on track and on time, and for being understanding and patient through the testy times. Her insightful eye and thoughtful analysis contributed to the consistency of the material.

- John Ribar, the technical editor, did a speedy-fine job of reviewing the material for accuracy, for which I am most grateful.

- Thanks also to Vivian Jaquette for a splendid job of copy editing the manuscript. Her insightful observations and comments contributed to the clarity and accuracy of the material.

- Finally, I want to thank Claire Splan, my project editor. She did an excellent job of herding this project through its final phases.

Introduction

Excel for Windows: The Pocket Reference puts the power of Excel 5 for Windows at your fingertips, seconds away from a quick refresher course on those commands, features, toolbars, and functions that you can't quite remember, or haven't used yet. Excel users of all types and skill levels—including beginning, intermediate, advanced, as well as on-again off-again users—will find this book a concise, comprehensive guide to accomplishing all kinds of spreadsheet tasks.

There are seven sections to this book. Section 1, "The Mechanics of Using Excel," provides an overview. You'll find a description of the Excel screen, reminders on how to work with Excel windows, mouse and keyboard instructions for moving around a workbook and a worksheet, useful tips and procedures for selecting text and objects, and various ways to access Excel menu and dialog box commands and options.

Sections 2 to 5 provide a quick reference to the features and commands necessary to create and work with a spreadsheet. Section 2, "Working with Workbooks and Worksheets," covers the tasks for building and manipulating a spreadsheet. Section 3, "Working with a Chart," covers creating and developing a chart. Section 4, "Working with a List," covers creating a list or a database. Section 5, "Working with Macros," gives a quick explanation of how to create a macro.

Each of these sections focuses on the features and commands specifically related to a task. References are listed alphabetically within each section. When looking for help with completing a task, first determine the section appropriate to that task, then look up the needed reference within that section. Individual references include a brief description of the task or feature, step-by-step instructions for accomplishing the task or activating the feature, a brief discussion of important options, and occasional notes that highlight important warnings or tips. If you have trouble locating a specific reference for a particular task, please refer to the index at the back of this book.

Section 6, "Toolbar Reference," contains information about the Excel toolbars. You'll find pictures of the buttons found on each toolbar and brief descriptions of how each button is used.

Section 7, "Excel Functions," contains an alphabetical list of Excel functions. The list contains the name of each function, the function arguments, and a short description of what the function returns.

Excel for Windows: The Pocket Reference is an excellent reference companion to your Excel documentation. This book will save you a great deal of time searching for and reading through the more detailed explanations found in the documentation. As a matter of fact, when you need help with an Excel feature, you may want to start here first, and then refer to the documentation when you need more detailed information.

The Mechanics of Using Excel 5

This chapter is a handy guide to the basics for using Excel 5 for Windows. You'll find a description of the components of the Excel application and workbook windows and of an Excel dialog box. You'll also find instructions for using a mouse and the keyboard to select menu items, commands, options, and chart objects; for selecting ranges of worksheet cells; for editing text and values; and for maneuvering around a worksheet.

THE APPLICATION AND WORKBOOK WINDOWS

There are two types of Excel windows, the *application window* and the *workbook window*; both are shown in Figure 1. A workbook window is contained within the borders of the application window. You can open more than one workbook at a time. Worksheets are organized within each workbook window.

Note *If the workbook window is maximized, it will fill the entire screen. The main menu bar, toolbars, formula bar, and status bar remain on the screen.*

SELECTING A NEW WORKSHEET IN A WORKBOOK

To select another worksheet in a workbook window, click on the worksheet scroll arrows located in the lower-left corner of the workbook window until the sheet number or name appears. Then click on the desired sheet number or

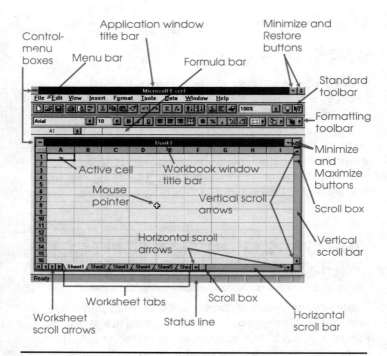

Figure 1-1 The Application and Workbook Windows

name. You can also press CTRL-PGDN or CTRL-PGUP to move forward or backward through the sheet numbers.

MOVING AROUND IN A WORKSHEET

Moving with the Mouse

To move the active cell to another location, move the mouse pointer to the desired cell and click the left mouse button. That cell becomes the active cell.

To look at another area of the worksheet without moving the active cell, click on the vertical or horizontal scroll arrows or on the scroll bar.

Moving with the Keyboard

The following table shows you how to move the active cell when using the keyboard:

Movement	Keypress
One cell right	RIGHT ARROW
One cell left	LEFT ARROW
One cell up	UP ARROW
One cell down	DOWN ARROW
To the beginning of a row	HOME
To cell A1	CTRL-HOME
To the cell where the far right column intersects the last row of data	CTRL-END
Down one screen	PGDN
Up one screen	PGUP
Upward to the last cell containing data before and after an empty cell	CTRL-UP ARROW
Downward to the last cell containing data before and after an empty cell	CTRL-DOWN ARROW
Right to the next cell containing data before and after an empty cell	CTRL-RIGHT ARROW
Left to the next cell containing data before and after an empty cell	CTRL-LEFT ARROW
To a specified cell or range of cells	F5

SELECTING MENU ITEMS, COMMANDS, CELLS, AND OBJECTS

You can use either a mouse or the keyboard to select pull-down menus, menu commands, cell ranges, and chart objects. The mouse is generally the fastest and easiest method when selecting items, but the keyboard is sometimes even faster, especially when you use a *hot key* or a *shortcut key*. The hot key is the underlined letter in a menu-item name or command name. A shortcut key allows you to press a single key or a combination of keys to bypass the menu system. Shortcut keys are displayed next to the menu item on the pull-down menus.

Note   *Another first-rate way to avoid the main menu bar is to display a shortcut menu. To do this, place the mouse pointer over a specific area of the screen and click the right mouse button. A menu pops up on the screen and provides commonly used options that correspond to the type of operations associated with that area of the screen. The shortcut menu items vary, depending on whether you are working in a worksheet, a chart, or a macro sheet.*

Selecting with a Mouse

The following table shows you how to move the active cell when using a mouse. It is assumed that your mouse is set up for a right-handed user; therefore, when instructed to click, you should click the left mouse button unless instructed specifically to click the right mouse button.

Note   *When instructed to drag the mouse, place the mouse pointer on an item, press and hold down the left mouse button, and drag the mouse pointer to a new location.*

Selection	Mouse Action
A pull-down menu item	Place the mouse pointer on the name of the menu item and click.
A command from a pull-down menu	Place the mouse pointer on the name of the command and click.
A cell	Click on the cell. A small square called a *handle* will appear in the lower-right corner of a cell.
A range of adjacent cells	Drag the mouse pointer over the cells.

Selection	Mouse Action
A group of nonadjacent cells	Press the CTRL key while selecting the cells.
An object	Place the mouse pointer on the object and click. Small squares called *handles* will appear around an object.
A group of objects	Press the SHIFT key while selecting the objects.
An entire row or column	Click on the row number or column letter.
Multiple rows or columns	Drag the mouse pointer over the row numbers or column letters.
The entire worksheet	Click the gray rectangle directly above the row numbers and to the left of the column letters.

Note *To unselect any selected area, click anywhere on the worksheet.*

Selecting Items with the Keyboard

To select menu items, commands, chart objects, or cells from the keyboard, use the following keys:

Selection	Keypress
A pull-down menu	Press ALT to activate the main menu bar. Then press the underlined hot key in the menu name. (Press ESC twice to close a pull-down menu and return to the workbook.)
An item from a pull-down menu	Highlight the item and press ENTER, or press the underlined menu hot key in the menu name.
An item using a shortcut key	Press the function key combination displayed next to the item name on the pull-down menu. Keys separated by a + mean to press and hold the first key and then press the second key.

Selection	Keypress
A chart object	Press CTRL, hold it down, press either the right or the left arrow key, and then release the CTRL key. Handles will appear around the object. (Press any arrow key to move the handles from object to object.)
Any number of cells while moving around the worksheet	Press SHIFT, hold it down, and press any movement key. (See the section MOVING AROUND IN A WORKSHEET.)
Nonadjacent cells	Select the first group of cells. Then press SHIFT-F8 (Add mode) and select additional groups of cells. To turn Add mode off, press SHIFT-F8 again.
An entire column	Press CTRL-SPACEBAR.
An entire row	Press SHIFT-SPACEBAR.
An entire worksheet	Press SHIFT-CTRL-SPACEBAR.
A specified range of cells	Press F5 and enter the cell address, range, or range name.

Moving Within a Selected Area

Do *not* attempt to use the cursor-movement keys to move around in the selected area of the worksheet. If you try, you will unselect the selected area. Instead, use the following keys:

Movement	Keypress
One cell to the right, row by row	TAB
One cell to the left, row by row	SHIFT-TAB
Down one cell, column by column	ENTER
Up one cell, column by column	SHIFT-ENTER

Movement	Keypress
To the next selected area	TAB, SHIFT-TAB, ENTER, or SHIFT-ENTER continuously to move to the end of one selected area and right into the next selected area.
Unselect the area and return to the active cell	SHIFT-BACKSPACE

WORKING WITH DIALOG BOXES

When you select a menu item that is followed by ellipses (...), a *dialog box* will appear on your screen. You can then choose from among the several options that appear in the dialog box. A dialog box is similar to a window in that it has a control-menu box and a title bar, and like a window it can be repositioned on the screen.

The following two illustrations show the components you'll find in an Excel dialog box:

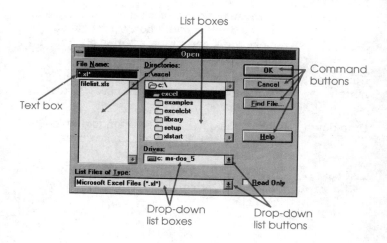

Option (radio) buttons   Option tabs   Command buttons

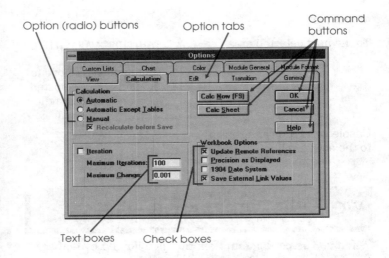

Text boxes   Check boxes

Selecting Dialog Box Items with a Mouse

The following table shows you how to select dialog box items using the mouse.

Selection	Mouse Action
Check box	To turn an option on, click the option name to place an X in the check box. Click again to remove the X and turn the option off. You may choose more than one item.
Command button	Click on a command button to immediately execute an action or, in some cases, to display another dialog box.
Drop-down list box	Click on the down-arrow button to drop down a list of choices. Then click on the desired item.
List box	To select an item in a list, double-click on the item. Items with grayed-out names are not available.

Selection	Mouse Action
Option button	To choose an item, click on the item name. The button will darken, indicating that the item has been selected. You can choose only one item from a common list of option buttons (often called *radio buttons*).
Option tab	To choose a tab, click on the name of the tab.

Selecting Dialog Box Items with the Keyboard

Using the mouse is without question the best method for selecting options in a dialog box, but the keyboard can also be used.

Action	Keypress
Move forward from item to item	TAB
Move backward from item to item	SHIFT-TAB
Select or deselect check boxes	SPACEBAR
Select a command button	ENTER
Close a dialog box without any action	ESC
Select or deselect a check box, or select a command button or radio button	Hold down the ALT key and press the hot key.
Select a tab	Hold down the CTRL key and press TAB.

Note   *The current command button will have either a dark border around it or a dark border along with a dotted line around the name on the button. Pressing ENTER will select the current command button.*

USING WINDOW AND DOCUMENT CONTROL MENUS

The control-menu boxes for the application and workbook windows are the gray boxes located in the upper-left corner of each window (see Figure 1). Each box has a small, horizontal bar in it. Selecting one of these boxes will pull down a menu with commands that allow you to move, size, and close the windows; switch between currently active Windows programs; and cycle through open Excel workbooks. This section discusses each command found on the application and workbook control menus.

Selecting a Control Menu

The application control menu is the box with the longest horizontal bar. The workbook control menu has the shorter bar. To select the application or workbook control menu with the mouse, click on the appropriate control menu box. If you use the keyboard, press ALT-SPACEBAR to select the application control menu, and press ALT-HYPHEN to display the workbook control menu. If you pull down a control menu and change your mind, click anywhere on the screen or press ESC twice to close the control menu and return to your document.

Options on the Application Control Menu

The following table describes how to use each option found on the application control menu. These options affect only the application window, not the document windows.

Action	Control Menu Option
Close the window and exit Excel	Select Close. To bypass the control menu, double-click on the control-menu box or press ALT-F4.
Minimize the window	Select Minimize. To bypass the control menu, click on the Minimize button (down arrow in the upper-right corner of the window). The application becomes an icon at the bottom of the Windows screen.
Maximize the window	Double-click on the minimized icon or press CTRL-ESC, select Microsoft Excel, and press ENTER. If the application window is windowed in the Windows environment, select the control menu and select Maximize. To bypass the control menu, click on the Maximize button (up arrow in the upper-right corner of the window).
Restore the window to its previous size and location	Select Restore or click on the Restore button (box with both up and down arrows in the upper-right corner of the window).
Move a window	Click on the title bar and drag the window to the new location. With the keyboard, press ALT-SPACEBAR and select Move. Then press the arrow keys to move the window (hold down CTRL to move in smaller increments) and press ENTER to anchor it in place.
Size a window	Place the mouse pointer on the window border. The pointer turns into a two-headed arrow. Now drag the window border to the desired position. From the keyboard, press ALT-SPACEBAR, select Size, and use the arrow keys to size the window (hold CTRL down to size in smaller increments). Press ENTER when the window is the appropriate size.

Action	Control Menu Option
Switch to another application	Select Switch to, or press CTRL-ESC to bypass the control menu. The Task List dialog box appears. Double-click on the application you want to switch to, or highlight it and press ENTER.

Options on the Document Control Menu

This section describes how to select options from the document control menu. These options only affect the window of the currently displayed workbook.

Action	Control Menu Option
Close a window	Select Close. To bypass the control menu, double-click on the control-menu box or press CTRL-F4.
Minimize a window	Select Minimize. To bypass the control menu, click on the Minimize button (upper-right corner of the window) or press CTRL-F9. The document window becomes an icon at the bottom of the application window.
Maximize a window	Double-click on the document icon or press ALT-HYPHEN and select Maximize. To bypass the control menu, press CTRL-F10.
Restore a minimized window to its previous size and location	Click on the icon and select Restore. To bypass the control menu, press CTRL-F5. (Press ALT-ESC to move from one minimized icon to another.)

Action	Control Menu Option
Move a window	Click on the title bar and drag the window to the new location. With the keyboard, press ALT-HYPHEN and select <u>M</u>ove, or press CTRL-F7 to bypass the control menu. Then press the arrow keys to move the window (hold down CTRL to move in smaller increments) and press ENTER to anchor it in place.
Size a window	Place the mouse pointer on the window border. The pointer turns into a two-headed arrow. Now drag the window border to the desired position. From the keyboard, press ALT-HYPHEN and select <u>S</u>ize, or press CTRL-F8. Then use the arrow keys to size the window (hold CTRL down to size in smaller increments) and press ENTER when the window is the appropriate size.
Change to the next open workbook window	Select Ne<u>x</u>t Window. To bypass the control menu, press CTRL-TAB.

Working with Workbooks and Worksheets

This section provides an alphabetical listing of the features available to you when working with Excel workbooks and worksheets.

ADD-INS

Add-ins provide functions and options to meet specific needs. Add-ins are installed with the Excel Setup program. Once an add-in is installed, it will appear on an Excel menu only if it has been activated.

Adding an Add-In to a Menu

To add an add-in to a pull-down menu and then activate it:

1. Select Tools | Add-Ins. The Add-Ins dialog box appears with a list of available add-ins.

2. If the add-in you want is not on the list, select Browse to look for the add-in filename in another directory or drive. Highlight the filename and select OK to add the add-in to the list. Add-in filenames have an .XLA or .XLL extension.

3. Place an X in the box in front of each add-in you want to use.

4. Select OK or press ENTER. The menu name for each selected add-in will appear on the appropriate pull-down menu.

Note   *If an add-in does not appear on the Add-Ins dialog box, run the Excel Setup program and install it.*

ADDRESSES

Cell addresses are used when constructing formulas. A cell address refers to a specific cell and the data within that cell. There are three types of references: absolute, relative, and mixed.

Absolute Reference
An *absolute reference* is entered with a dollar sign ($) in front of the row and column designator, for example A1. An absolute reference will always refer to the designated cell whenever its formula is copied to another location.

Relative Reference
A *relative reference* is entered with only the cell row and column designator, for example A1. A relative reference will change relative to where its formula is copied.

Mixed Reference
A *mixed reference* is entered with a dollar sign ($) preceding either the row or column designator, for example A$1 or $A1. This type of reference is therefore a mixture of an absolute reference and a relative reference. When a formula containing a mixed reference is copied to a new location, the relative portion of the reference will change relative to the new row or column, and the absolute portion of the reference will always refer to the same row or column regardless of the new location.

ALIGNING CELL DATA

To set the alignment for a range of cells:

1. Select the range of cells to be aligned.
2. Select Format | Style to display the Style dialog box and then select Modify, or click the right mouse button on

the selected cells and select Format Cells. The Format Cells dialog box appears.

3. Select the Alignment tab and choose the appropriate alignment options. (See the following sections, "Horizontal Alignment Options" and "Vertical Alignment Options.")

4. Select OK or press ENTER once or twice, depending on how you arrived at the Format Cells dialog box. The alignment options are applied to the selected cells.

Horizontal Alignment Options

General (default)
Text is aligned left, numbers are placed flush-right, and logical and error values are centered in the cells.

Left, Center, Right
Cell data is aligned left, center, or flush-right in the selected cells.

Fill
Repeats a cell entry across the width of the cell. Selected blank cells to the right of the cell with data are also filled. The value of the cell is unaffected.

Justify
Text is aligned between the left and right edge of the cell when the Wrap Text box is checked.

Center across selection
Centers data in a cell across the selected cells.

Wrap Text
Check this box to have text wrap between the edges of the cell (similar to word-wrap in a word processor). If you edit the length of the text, you may need to change the row height.

Vertical Alignment Options

Top, Center, Bottom
Data is aligned with the top, center, or bottom of a cell.

Orientation Alignment Options

Select the box that shows an example of how you want your text to appear. You may need to adjust the height of the row to accommodate the increased vertical length of rotated text.

ANALYSIS TOOLPAK

The Analysis Toolpak contains various tools that perform engineering, statistical, and financial functions.

Accessing the Analysis Toolpak

To gain access to the Analysis Toolpak:

1. Select Tools | Data Analysis to display a list of engineering and statistical tools.
2. Choose the appropriate tool from the list and select OK or press ENTER.
3. Enter the desired options for the selected tool.
4. Select OK or press ENTER.

Note   *The Data Analysis command will not appear on the Tools menu unless the Analysis Toolpak add-in has been installed on the hard drive and activated. See ADD-INS, "Adding an Add-In to a Menu," for instructions on adding an add-in to a pull-down menu.*

AUDITING DATA

Trace the source of problems involving data and formula entries. Trace arrows are projected over the data to and from cell values that are dependent on each other for supporting information.

Tracing Precedent Values

This feature draws arrows from all cells, called *precedents*, that supply values directly to the formula in the active cell. The active cell must contain a formula for this command to work.

1. Select the active cell containing a formula.
2. Select Tools | Auditing | Trace Precedents, or click on the Trace Precedents button on the Auditing toolbar. An arrow appears over the cells contributing values that affect the formula.
3. You can repeat Step 2 to draw arrows to additional levels of precedents.

Tracing Dependent Formulas

This feature draws arrows from the active cell to all cells that contain formulas, called *dependents*, that are dependent on the value in the active cell. The value in the active cell must be used by a formula or this feature will not work.

1. Select an active cell containing a value that is used by a formula in another cell.
2. Select Tools | Auditing | Trace Dependents, or click on the Trace Dependents button on the Auditing toolbar. Arrows appear that lead from the active cell to the formulas dependent on the value in the active cell.
3. You can repeat Step 2 to draw arrows to additional levels of dependents.

Tracing Errors

Draws arrows from an active cell containing an error value to the cells that may have caused the error. This command will not work unless the active cell contains an error value.

1. Select the active cell that contains an error value.
2. Select Tools | Auditing | Trace Error, or click on the Trace Error button on the Auditing toolbar. A red or

dotted arrow points from the active cell to the first error value. A blue or solid arrow might point to an error value that somehow affected the first error value.

3. The cell containing the error is automatically selected so that you can analyze the problem and repair it.

Removing Trace Arrows

Clear away trace arrows that obscure important data on the worksheet. You can remove all the arrows, just the dependent arrows, or just the precedent arrows.

1. To remove all the arrows, select Tools | Auditing | Remove All Arrows, or click on the Remove All Arrows button on the Auditing toolbar. The arrows disappear from the worksheet.

2. To remove only the dependent arrows, click on the Remove Dependent Arrows button on the Auditing toolbar.

3. To remove only the precedent arrows, click on the Remove Precedent Arrows button on the Auditing toolbar.

BORDERS

See FORMAT, "Adding Borders Around Cells."

CALCULATING ALL OPEN DOCUMENTS

To control the calculations of active documents:

1. Select Tools | Options. The Options dialog box appears.

2. Select the Calculation tab, and then select the appropriate options.

3. Select Calc Now or press F9 to calculate all open documents, or select Calc Sheet to calculate only the active document. You can recalculate a worksheet at any time by pressing F9.

4. If you only want to select options and do not need to calculate, select OK or press ENTER to return to the worksheet.

Calculation Options

Automatic
Automatically recalculates a document.

Automatic Except Tables
Automatically recalculates a document except for formulas within tables. To calculate tables, select Calc Now or Calc Sheet.

Manual
Recalculation only occurs when you press F9 or select Calc Now or Calc Sheet.

Recalculate before Save
This option is only available when Manual recalculation is selected. The worksheet will automatically recalculate when it is saved.

Iteration
Check the Iterations check box if you want to specify the Maximum Iterations and Maximum Change constraint for an iteration.

Update Remote References
When this option is turned on, formulas that contain remote references are updated at each recalculation.

Precision as Displayed
When this option is turned on, the accuracy of a calculation is limited to how the value is displayed in the cell. When turned off, accuracy is calculated out to 15 digits.

1904 Date System
When this option is turned on, dates are calculated according to the 1904 system. When turned off, dates are calculated according to the 1900 system.

Save External Link Values
When this option is turned on, the values in a linked document are saved along with the worksheet.

CELLS

Centering Data in a Cell

See ALIGNING CELL DATA.

Clearing Data from a Cell

To clear data from selected cells:

1. Select a single cell or a range of cells.
2. Select Edit | Clear to display a pop-up menu.
3. Select the item you want cleared from the selected cells.

Note DEL *is the shortcut key for clearing only the contents of a cell. You can also click the right mouse button on the selected cells to display the Shortcut menu and select Clear Contents.*

Clear Options
All
Removes all formats, contents, and notes.

Formats
Removes only the cell formatting, returning the cell to the default General format. See the information on the Clear Formats toolbar button in the "Toolbar Reference" section.

Contents
Removes only the cell contents, leaving all formatting and notes in place. See the information on the Clear Contents toolbar button in the "Toolbar Reference" section.

Notes
Removes only the cell notes, leaving formats and contents unaffected.

Deleting a Cell

See DELETING CELLS, COLUMNS, AND ROWS.

CLOSING AN ACTIVE WORKBOOK

To close only the active workbook:

1. Select File | Close.
2. If the latest changes to any of the worksheets in the workbook have not been saved, you are asked if you want to save the workbook.
3. Select Yes to save, No to close without saving, or Cancel (ESC) to cancel the Close operation and keep the workbook open.

Closing All Active Workbooks

This feature is used when you have more than one active workbook and want to close them all in one operation. To close all active documents at once:

1. Press SHIFT, hold it down, and select File | Close All.
2. If the latest changes to any active workbook have not been saved, you are asked if you want to save them.
3. Select Yes to save, No to close a workbook without saving, or Cancel (ESC) to cancel the Close operation completely, leaving all the workbooks open. Any

workbook that was saved prior to cancelling the command remains saved.

COLOR

Modifying Workbook Colors

You can modify colors for text, objects, cells, gridlines, fills, and fonts.

To customize the display colors for a workbook:

1. Select Tools | Options, and then select the Color tab.
2. Click on the desired color. A gray box appears around the selected color.
3. To modify the color, select Modify. The Color Picker dialog box appears.
4. Edit the color by typing new values in the appropriate boxes, by clicking on the up and down arrows in the option boxes, or by dragging the small, white triangle up and down along the vertical color bar. Select OK when done.
5. If you're not satisfied with a modified color, select Reset to return to the original color.
6. To copy the colors from another workbook, select Copy Colors from and drop down the list of open workbooks. Select a workbook from the list.
7. Select OK or press ENTER when finished.

COLUMNS

Deleting a Column

See DELETING CELLS, COLUMNS, AND ROWS.

Hiding, Unhiding, and Changing Column Width

To hide and unhide columns or change their width:

1. Select at least one cell in each column for which you want to hide or change the width. If you want to change the column width for more than one worksheet at the same time, select each worksheet (see SELECTING, "Selecting Two or More Worksheets in a Workbook").

2. Select Format | Column to display the Column menu.

3. Select Hide to set the width of the selected columns to zero, causing the columns to disappear from the worksheet. The cell data is unaffected. You can restore the hidden columns by selecting two cells from columns on adjacent sides of the hidden columns and then selecting Format | Unhide.

4. Select AutoFit Selection to expand the selected columns to fit the widest cell in each column. A shortcut to expand a column for the best fit is to double-click on the right-side border of the column head.

5. To specify a width for the column, select Width. The Column Width dialog box appears. The standard width of a column is 8.43 characters, based on the original default font.

6. In the Column Width box, type a number (decimal fractions are allowed) from 0 to 255. Then select OK or press ENTER.

7. If you are not satisfied with the new column width, select Format | Column | Standard Width. Make sure the Standard Column Width box is the size you want and then select OK or press ENTER.

Note *You can bypass the menu selections and change column width with the mouse by placing the mouse pointer on the right-side border of the column heading. The pointer turns into a two-headed arrow that you can drag to the desired column width.*

CONSOLIDATING DATA

Consolidate one or more source values into a table located in a destination area on a worksheet. The source values can be in the same worksheet, in other worksheets, or in other workbooks. You can consolidate by *category* or by *position*. Excel defines a category of source values as those values associated with worksheet labels. Position values are associated with worksheet cells.

1. Determine the locations of the source data you want to consolidate. Sources can be on one worksheet, on several worksheets, or in several workbooks.

2. Select the destination area of the worksheet where the consolidation will take place. This area can be a cell, a range of cells, a column, or a row.

3. Select Data | Consolidate. The Consolidate dialog box appears.

4. Select Function and choose a function from the drop-down menu to be used to calculate the consolidation. The default function is SUM.

5. In the Reference box, type in the location of one of the source values. (If the source worksheet is open, click on it and select the source area. Include category labels if doing a category consolidation.)

Source locations can be entered as follows:

Situation	Information to Enter
Destination and sources are on the same worksheet.	Cell references
Destination and sources are on different worksheets.	Sheet name and cell references
Destination and sources are in different workbooks.	Book name, sheet name, and cell references

Situation	Information to Enter
Destination and sources are in different workbooks in different locations on the disk.	Full path, book name, sheet name, and cell references
The source area is named.	Name of the source area

Note   *You can consolidate up to 255 source areas. Source worksheets are not required to be open during consolidation. You should save any unsaved source worksheet before performing a consolidation.*

6. After the source area is entered, click on <u>A</u>dd.
7. Repeat steps 5 and 6 for each source area you want consolidated.
8. Select OK or press ENTER.

Note   *When consolidating values identically positioned on their respective worksheets, do not include cells containing text labels, and double-check that the values in each source area are located in the same cells on each worksheet.*

Consolidate Options

<u>B</u>rowse
Select <u>B</u>rowse to select the source file from a directory listing. Then type the cell reference or name for the source area after the filename.

Create Links to <u>S</u>ource Data
When selected, the consolidation value will automatically be updated if a source value changes.

<u>T</u>op Row, <u>L</u>eft Column
When consolidating by *category*, select one or both of these options if there are labels in the top row and/or left column. Excel consolidates by *position* for any box that is left unchecked.

<u>D</u>elete
Delete the highlighted source from the All R<u>e</u>ferences list.

COPYING AND PASTING DATA

Copy selected data from one location to another. To copy data into the same worksheet, to another workbook or worksheet, or to another application:

1. Select the cell or range of cells that contains the data to be copied.

2. To copy, either select Edit | Copy; press CTRL-C; click on the Copy button on the Standard toolbar; or click the right mouse button and select Copy. A marquee appears around the selection.

3. Select the destination location.

4. To paste, either select Edit | Paste; click the right mouse button and select Paste; press CTRL-V or ENTER; or click on the Paste button on the Standard toolbar.

Note *The copied information will overwrite any cell that contains data, so be sure to select a clear area of the worksheet that is large enough to handle a large range of copied information.*

COPYING A PICTORIAL REPRESENTATION

To copy a pictorial representation of selected data to be used in another application, such as a word processor, or in an Excel worksheet:

1. Select the range of data to be copied as a picture.

2. Press SHIFT and select Edit | Copy Picture, or press ALT, SHIFT-E, C. The Copy Picture dialog box appears.

3. Select As Shown On Screen to paste the selection into an Excel worksheet. Select As Shown When Printed to paste the selection into another application.

4. Select the Picture or Bitmap format depending on the type of graphic.

5. Select OK or press ENTER to copy the picture to the Clipboard.

6. To insert the picture, either select the destination location and select Edit | Paste; press SHIFT and select Edit | Paste Picture; or click on the Paste button on the Standard toolbar.

Note   *The Camera button on the Standard toolbar is a fast way to create and paste a pictorial representation from one workbook or worksheet to another. Select the cells to be turned into a picture, click on the Camera button, and then click on the worksheet where you want the picture to appear. Presto! You have a pictorial representation of the selected cells.*

CUTTING AND PASTING DATA

Move data from one location to another, deleting the data from the original location. You can move data to another location in the same worksheet or workbook, or to another application.

A fast method of moving data from one location to another is to select the cells, place the mouse pointer on the border of the selection, and drag the border to the destination area. Here is another method:

1. Select the range of data to be moved.

2. Select Edit | Cut; press CTRL-X; click the right mouse button on the range and select Cut; or click on the Cut button on the Standard toolbar. A marquee appears around the data to be moved.

3. Select the destination cell and select Edit | Paste; click the right mouse button and select Paste; press CTRL-V or ENTER; or click on the Paste button on the Standard toolbar.

Note   *The copied information will overwrite any cell that contains data, so be sure to select a clear area of the worksheet that is large enough to handle a large range of pasted data.*

DATE FORMATTING

See NUMBERS, DATES, AND TIME VALUES, "Modifying the Appearance of Numbers, Dates, and Time Values."

DEFAULT SETTINGS

To modify the General default settings:

1. Select Tools | Options. The Options dialog box appears.
2. Select the General tab.
3. Select the desired default settings (see the following section, "General Default Settings").
4. Select OK or press ENTER when satisfied with the settings.

General Default Settings

A1 or R1C1
Displays cell references in the A1 or R1C1 format.

Recently Used File List
Check this box to display the four most recently opened files on the File menu.

Microsoft Excel 4.0 Menus
Check this box to display the Excel 4.0 menus.

Ignore Other Applications
Check this box to ignore any request made by other applications using Dynamic Data Exchange (DDE).

Prompt For Summary Info

Check this box to display the Summary Info dialog box when you save a new workbook.

Reset TipWizard

Check this box to have the TipWizard show you some tips you may have already seen.

Sheets In New Workbook

Click on the up or down arrow, or type in a number, to set the default number of worksheets in a new workbook.

Standard Font

Select the default font from the drop-down list.

Size

Select the default font size from the drop-down list.

Default File Location

Type the path for the default working directory.

Alternate Startup File Location

Type the path to the alternate startup directory.

User Name

Type the name you want to see displayed in views, scenarios, summary information, and file sharing.

DELETING CELLS, COLUMNS, AND ROWS

Delete selected cells, rows, and columns and all data within the selected area. Cells around the deleted area will shift to fill in the vacated space.

1. Select the range of cells to be deleted.
2. Select Edit | Delete; press CTRL-HYPHEN; or click the right mouse button on the range and select Delete. The

Delete dialog box appears. If you selected a row or column in Step 1, the cells are immediately deleted and the surrounding cells automatically adjust to fill the deleted space.

3. Select the appropriate delete option.
4. Select OK or press ENTER to delete the range.

Note *Be careful! The Edit | Delete command deletes not only the data in a cell, but also the cell itself. Do not confuse this command with the Edit | Clear command.*

DELETING A FILE

To delete a file from the disk:

1. Select File | Find File. The Find File dialog box appears.
2. Select the appropriate drive and directory, and the file or files to be deleted.
3. Select the Commands button.
4. Select Delete. You are asked if you want to delete the selected file, in case you decide to change your mind.
5. Select Yes or press ENTER.
6. Select Close or press ESC to close the Find File dialog box.

DELETING A WORKSHEET FROM A WORKBOOK

To delete one or more worksheets from a workbook:

1. Select the worksheet to be deleted.
2. Select Edit | Delete Sheet. You are asked if you want to delete the worksheets permanently.
3. Select OK or press ENTER to delete the worksheets.

DELETING AN OBJECT

See OBJECTS, "Removing a Chart Object," in the "Working with a Chart" section.

DISPLAY DEFAULT SETTINGS

To specify the default settings that control which screen elements are displayed when you start Excel:

1. Select Tools | Options to display the Options dialog box.
2. Select the View tab.
3. Select from the following View settings to establish the default settings for the Excel screen elements.
4. Select OK or press ENTER when finished.

View Settings

Formula Bar
Check to display or hide the formula bar.

Status Bar
Check to display or hide the status bar at the bottom of the application window.

Note Indicator
Check to display or hide a small red dot in the upper-right corner of cells that contain notes.

Info Window
Check to display or hide the Info window.

Show All
Select to display graphic and drawn objects, buttons, pictures, and text boxes.

Show Placeholders
Select to display selected pictures and charts as gray rectangles. Objects, text boxes, and buttons are not affected.

Hide All
Select to hide all graphic and drawn objects, buttons, pictures, and text boxes. Hidden objects will not be printed.

Automatic Page Breaks
Check to display the automatic page breaks set by Excel.

Formulas
Check to display cell formulas instead of the values produced.

Gridlines
Check to display cell gridlines.

Color
Select a gridline and column and row heading color from the drop-down list.

Row & Column Headers
Check to display row and column headings.

Outline Symbols
Check to display outlining symbols on an outlined worksheet.

Zero Values
Check to display all zero values. If not checked, cells that have zero values are displayed as blank cells. If you use the Number tab in the Format Cells dialog box and format cells to display zeros, those cells are not affected.

Horizontal Scroll Bar
Check to display the horizontal scroll bar.

Vertical Scroll Bar
Check to display the vertical scroll bar.

Sheet Tabs
Check to display worksheet tabs.

DRAWING SHAPES

Draw basic rectangles, ovals, arcs, and arrows. Drawings can be sized, formatted, and repositioned like any other graphic object.

1. Display the Drawing toolbar (*see* TOOLBARS, "Displaying and Hiding a Toolbar," for instructions on displaying a toolbar.)

2. Select the appropriate drawing button from the Drawing toolbar.

3. Drag the mouse to create the drawing.

4. To change the shape of the drawing, click on the Reshape button and drag the handles to the desired shape.

5. To delete a drawing, click on it to select it and then press DEL.

Note *When drawing with the Freehand Polygon button, you must double-click the mouse to stop drawing after the drawing is completed.*

EDITING CELL DATA

If information in a cell needs to be changed, you can start from scratch and reenter all the data. It is easier to use the Edit mode, however, for long entries where there are only a few edits to be made.

Editing Data in a Cell

To edit the data in a cell:

1. Select the cell that contains the data to be edited.
2. Press F2 to enter the Edit mode. The insertion point appears in the cell at the end of the cell data.
3. Edit the data directly in the cell. To cancel an edit, click on the X button on the formula bar, or press ESC.
4. Press ENTER or click on the ✓ button on the formula bar when the edits have been completed.

Moving the Insertion Point While Editing

The following table shows you how to move the insertion point when editing data in a cell.

Movement	Keypress
One character left or right	LEFT ARROW or RIGHT ARROW
One line up or down	UP ARROW or DOWN ARROW
To the beginning of a line	HOME
To the end of a line	END
One word to the left	CTRL-LEFT ARROW
One word to the right	CTRL-RIGHT ARROW

Deleting Data While Editing

This table shows you how to delete incorrect data.

Deletion	Keypress
The character to the right of the insertion point	DEL
The character to the left of the insertion point	BACKSPACE
All characters from the insertion point to the end of the line	CTRL-DEL

EDIT DEFAULT SETTINGS

To specify the default settings that control many of the editing features available in Excel:

1. Select Tools | Options to display the Options dialog box.
2. Select the Edit tab.
3. Select from the Edit settings (see the following section, "Edit Settings") to establish the default edit settings.
4. Select OK or press ENTER when finished.

Edit Settings

Edit Directly in Cell
Check to edit directly inside a cell by double-clicking on the cell.

Allow Cell Drag and Drop
Check to move and copy cells by dragging them to a new location using the mouse.

Alert Before Overwriting Cells
Check to display a warning before copying cells over cells that already contain data.

Move Selection after Enter
Check to have the active cell automatically move down one row after pressing ENTER to enter data in a cell.

Fixed Decimal
Check to automatically insert a decimal point into numerical values according to the number entered in the Places box.

Cut, Copy, and Sort Objects with Cells
Check to keep objects with cells that are copied, cut, filtered, or sorted.

Ask to Update Automatic Links
Check to display a dialog box asking if you want to update OLE links to other applications.

EXITING EXCEL

To close all open documents and exit the program:

1. Select File | Exit or press ALT-F4. A dialog box prompts you to save any documents that have been changed but have not been saved.

2. Select Yes or No to save or not save the open documents prior to exiting. Select Cancel (ESC) to keep all files open and remain in the program.

FILE MANAGEMENT

To find, copy, delete, sort, and open files located in any directory or drive:

1. Select File | Find File, or click on the Find File button on the WorkGroup toolbar, to display the Find File dialog box. A list of files that were found in the most recent search appears in the Listed Files box.

2. Drop down the View menu and select a view option (*see* "View Options").

3. To search for a file, select Search to display the Search dialog box (*see* "Search Options").

4. Once you have found the file, you can select options from the Commands menu (*see* "Commands Options").

5. Select Open to open the selected workbook, or select Close to return to the other workbook.

View Options

Summary

Displays the summary information you specified when saving the workbook.

File Info

Displays the title, size, and author of the selected workbook, as well as the date last saved.

Preview

Displays a visual preview of the upper-left corner of the selected active sheet in the selected workbook.

Search Options

Saved Searches

From the drop-down list, select a saved search and search the disk according to the saved search criteria.

Save Search As

Save the search criteria to be used in a future search.

Search For

Type a filename in the File Name box and select a drive to be searched in the Location box.

Clear

Clears all search entries.

Advanced Search

Select advanced search criteria from the Advanced Search dialog box. Select options from the Location, Summary, and Timestamp tabs.

Commands Options

Open Read Only

The selected file is opened in a read-only format. The file can be viewed, but not edited.

Print

Select the desired printing options.

Delete

Delete the selected workbooks.

Note   *You can print or delete a group of workbooks by selecting them in the Listed Files box prior to selecting Print or Delete.*

Copy

Display the Copy dialog box and type in the drive and directory where the selected workbooks will be copied. Select <u>N</u>ew if you want to create a new directory.

Sor<u>t</u>ing

Select various sorting criteria that will determine how the files found in a search operation will be listed.

FILLING DATA ACROSS WORKSHEETS

To copy a range of cells to the same cells in all the selected worksheets in a workbook:

1. Select a group of worksheets in the open workbook by holding down CTRL while clicking on the worksheet tabs.

2. Select the range of cells to be filled in the currently displayed worksheet. Be careful, because this same range will be filled on the selected worksheets, overwriting any existing data in that range.

3. Select <u>E</u>dit | F<u>i</u>ll | <u>A</u>cross Worksheets. The Fill Across Worksheets dialog box appears.

4. Select <u>A</u>ll to copy all data, formulas, and formats. Select <u>C</u>ontents to copy only the cell contents, or select Forma<u>t</u>s to copy only formats.

5. Select OK or press ENTER. The fill range will appear on each of the selected worksheets.

FILLING DATA IN A ROW OR COLUMN RANGE

Copy existing data into a selected range of cells in either a row or a column. You can copy left or right in a row and up or down in a column.

1. Select a range of cells to be filled. Data copied into a row must be located in the left-most or right-most cell. Data to be copied into a column range must be located in the top-most or bottom-most cell. Be careful, because the copied data will overwrite existing data in the selected range of cells.

2. Select Edit | Fill to display the Fill menu. To fill right or left in a row, select Right or Left. To fill up or down in a column, select Up or Down. To bypass the menu system completely, press CTRL-D for a Down fill or CTRL-R for a Right fill.

FINDING A CELL REFERENCE OR RANGE NAME

To locate a cell or range name:

1. Select Edit | Go To or press F5. The Go To dialog box is displayed.

2. Select Go To and choose a name from the list box, or select Reference and type a cell address or name in the box. (*See* SELECTING, "Selecting Cells with Special Characteristics," for a description of the Special button.)

3. Select OK or press ENTER.

Note   *The fastest way to locate a range is to click on the Range button (the down-arrow button on the formula bar). An alphabetical list appears with the names of all the ranges in the active worksheet. Click on a range name to move to that range. The range name appears on the formula bar to the left of the down-arrow button.*

FINDING SPECIFIED DATA

To locate the next occurrence of a specified number or text entry in a selected range or in the entire worksheet:

1. Select the range to be searched. If no range is selected, the entire worksheet will be searched.
2. Select Edit | Find or press CTRL-F. The Find dialog box appears.
3. Select Find What and type the text or number to be found.
4. Select the appropriate search options.
5. Select OK or press ENTER to initiate the search. The first occurrence of the number or text is found.
6. Select Find Next or press ENTER to find subsequent occurrences.

Options

Search
Search by rows or by columns.

Look in
Select either Formulas, Values, or Notes to specify which cells are to be searched.

Match Case
Mark the Match Case check box to find search data that matches both uppercase and lowercase characters.

Find Entire Cells Only
Mark the check box to find cells in which the contents exactly match the search data. Leave the box blank to find cells in which the search data is part of a string of text.

FONT

Changing a Font Style, Size, and Color

Greater attention is directed to text that somehow stands out from the surrounding text. Text can be enhanced by changing the font style, size, or color.

To enhance the appearance of text on a worksheet:

1. Select the range of cells to be enhanced.

2. Select Format | Cells; click the right mouse button on the selection and select Format Cells; or press CTRL-1. The Format Cells dialog box appears. Now select the Font tab.

3. Select a font from the Font list box, a font style from the Font Style list box, and a font size from the Size list box (type in a size if the size you want is not listed). A text sample appears in the Sample box.

4. Select the style of underlining from the Underline drop-down menu.

5. Turn on Strikethrough, Superscript, or Subscript if desired.

6. Drop down the Color list and select a new text color.

7. Select the Normal Font box when you change your mind about a font selection and want to return to the default font.

8. Select OK or press ENTER to apply the changes and close the dialog box.

FOOTERS

See FORMATTING A DOCUMENT, "Header/Footer Options."

FORMAT

This section contains information for enhancing the entire worksheet.

Adding Borders Around Cells

To enhance cell borders by adding lines:

1. Select the range of cells to be enhanced.
2. Select Format | Cells; click the right mouse button on the selected cells and select Format Cells; or press CTRL-1. The Format Cells dialog box appears.
3. Select the Border tab.
4. In the Border area, select where you want the border to appear. You can choose more than one option.
5. In the Style area, select the style for the border lines and a color from the Color drop-down list.
6. Select OK or press ENTER to apply the enhancements.

Applying a Cell Format Style

Apply a format style to the contents of a selected cell or cells. You must define a cell format style before you can apply it to a cell. *See* "Creating a Cell Format Style."

1. Select the cell or cells to which you want to apply a previously created format style.
2. Select Format | Style. The Style dialog box appears.
3. Drop down the Style Name list and select the desired style.
4. Select OK or press ENTER to apply the chosen style to the selected cell or cells.

Applying A Predefined Format

To apply a built-in format to a range of cells:

1. Select the range of cells to be formatted.
2. Select Format | AutoFormat to display the AutoFormat dialog box.

3. Select <u>T</u>able Format and choose a format from the list box. An example of the selected format appears in the Sample area.

4. Select <u>O</u>ptions to turn on or off specific formatting elements.

5. Select OK or press ENTER to apply the formats to the selected cells.

Creating A Cell Format Style

To create specific cell formats, define them as a *style* and assign the style a name. The style can then be applied to any cell or cells. You can create a style in two ways, by *example* and by *definition.*

Creating a Style by Example

1. Select a cell that contains the formatting options to be included in the style you are creating.

2. Select Forma<u>t</u> | <u>S</u>tyle to display the Style dialog box. The style elements currently active in the selected cells appear in the Style Includes area. Unselecting a check box will turn off that particular style element.

3. Type a new style name in the <u>S</u>tyle Name text box.

4. Select OK or press ENTER. The formats in the selected cell are now incorporated in the named style.

Creating a Style by Definition

1. Select Forma<u>t</u> | <u>S</u>tyle to display the Style dialog box.

2. Type a name in the <u>S</u>tyle Name text box. Do not press ENTER.

3. Select <u>M</u>odify. The Format Cells dialog box appears.

4. Select the tabs and formatting options you want to appear in the style.

5. Select OK or press ENTER when done. The style elements for the currently selected style appear in the Style Includes area. Unselecting any style-element check box turns off that particular element.

6. Select <u>A</u>dd to add the style to the style list.

7. Select OK or press ENTER to save the style.

Additional Options

Delete
Deletes the style appearing in the Style Name box.

Merge
Copies the style names from one open workbook to another. The merged styles will appear on the Style Name drop-down list.

Defining Cell Shadings

To place a background shading in selected cells:

1. Select a range of cells.
2. Select Format | Cells; click the right mouse button on the selected cells and select Format Cells; or press CTRL-1.
3. Select the Patterns tab to display the Patterns options.
4. Select the desired color in the Color area.
5. Select Pattern and click on the desired pattern, or press the arrow keys to select a pattern.
6. Select OK or press ENTER to apply the background shading to the selected cells.

FORMATTING A DOCUMENT

Modify the appearance of a worksheet prior to printing. Appearance options include margins, headers, footers, page orientation, scaling of the worksheet, centering, and size.

1. Select the worksheet or worksheets to be formatted.
2. Select File | Page Setup to display the Page Setup dialog box.
3. Select the appropriate tabs and options (see "Page Options") for your document.

4. Select OK or press ENTER to assign the settings to the document. When the document is saved, the settings are saved along with it.

Note *Any changes you make in the Page Setup dialog box will change the settings for all the selected worksheets in the workbook.*

Page Options

Orientation
Select the appropriate mode, Portrait or Landscape.

Scaling
Select the Adjust To option to specify the percentage of reduction or enlargement for a document. Select the Fit To option to compress the document (or a selection) during printing so that it will print on the specified number of pages.

Paper Size
Select one of several envelope and paper sizes.

Print Quality
Select the print resolution in dpi (dots per inch) from the drop-down list.

First Page Number
Enter the page number you wish to appear on the first printed page. Page numbering for the second and following sheets will go in ascending order from the number you chose for the first page.

Print
Sends the document to the printer and allows you to select the print range, print quality, number of copies, and speed of printing. Also lets you preview the document before printing.

Print Preview
View the document before it prints.

Options
Display a dialog box with options specific to the currently selected printer.

Margins Options

Margins
Select Left, Right, Top, and Bottom and type in the desired margins in inches, or click the up and down arrows to increase or decrease the size. Select Horizontally or Vertically to center the text between the margins.

Header and Footer
Enter the distance you want between the edge of the page and the headers and footers.

Header/Footer Options

Header/Footer
Select a built-in header or footer from the Header or Footer drop-down list.

Custom Header/Custom Footer
Create a custom header or footer by selecting a built-in header or footer, clicking on Custom Header or Custom Footer, and making the appropriate modifications.

Sheet Options

Print Area
Type in the cell references for the print range, or select the range directly off the worksheet by dragging the mouse over the desired area. You can select more than one print range at a time.

Print Titles
To print titles, enter the row and column ranges to be used for the titles in the Rows to Repeat at Top and the Columns to Repeat at Left boxes.

Gridlines
Check this box to print horizontal and vertical gridlines between cells.

Notes
Check this box to print worksheet notes on an additional page.

Draft Quality
Check this box to speed up the printing of a worksheet by using a lower resolution and not printing the gridlines.

Black & White
Check this box to print cells and text boxes in black and white without any patterns or color formats. Use this option when printing color graphics on a black-and-white printer.

Row & Column Headings
Check this box to print the row numbers and column letters on each page.

Page Order
Select Down and then Across, or Across and then Down, to control the order in which the worksheet data is printed. The small worksheet icon to the right of the options displays the order in which data will print on the page.

FORMULA BAR

Hiding and Viewing the Formula Bar

You can remove the formula bar from the application window and then display it when needed. This is helpful when you want to see more of the active worksheet.

1. To hide the formula bar, select View | Formula Bar. When the formula bar is displayed, there is a check

mark in front of the _F_ormula Bar menu command. The formula bar disappears from view.

2. To display the hidden formula bar, select _V_iew | _F_ormula Bar.

FORMULAS

Creating a Formula

See FUNCTION WIZARD, "Building a Formula."

Clearing a Formula from a Cell

See CELLS, "Clearing Data from a Cell."

FUNCTION WIZARD

The Function Wizard assists you in building formulas by helping construct the formula and providing important information about formula arguments.

Building a Formula

To select predefined functions and build a custom formula directly into a selected cell:

1. Select a cell where the formula will be pasted.

2. Select _I_nsert | _F_unction; click on the Function Wizard button on the Standard toolbar; or press SHIFT-F3. The first of two Function Wizard dialog boxes is displayed.

3. Select Function _C_ategory and choose the appropriate category of functions. The associated functions appear in the Function _N_ame list box.

4. Select Function _N_ame and choose the desired function. The function name appears in the selected cell and on the formula bar. Select _F_inish if you want to insert the

function without any arguments, but with argument descriptions.

5. To select arguments, select Next to display the second Function Wizard dialog box.

6. Type numbers, references, formulas, text, or functions in the argument boxes, or use the mouse to select the references directly on the worksheet. The value for the function appears in the Value box.

7. Select <u>F</u>inish to enter the function into the formula.

Note   *When typing a formula into a cell, press CTRL-A to display the second dialog box of the Function Wizard for help in completing the formula. You can also press CTRL-SHIFT-A to paste argument descriptions directly into the formula, where you can then edit them with actual arguments.*

GOAL SEEK

Goal Seek is an analysis tool designed to answer "what if" questions.

Analyzing a Solution by Changing a Variable

Analyze one formula to determine a value that will produce a hypothetical solution for a designated second formula. The question is this: What value must the selected variable have in order for the formula to calculate the result you've specified?

1. Select a cell containing the formula to be analyzed.

2. Select <u>T</u>ools | Goa<u>l</u> Seek. The Goal Seek dialog box is displayed. The cell address containing the formula appears in the <u>S</u>et Cell box.

3. Select To <u>v</u>alue and enter the hypothetical value you want the formula to produce.

4. Select By changing cell. Then click on the cell or type in the cell address that contains the variable to be analyzed.

5. Select OK or press ENTER to continue, or select Pause or Cancel to pause or cancel the operation.

6. Select OK or press ENTER to change the old values on the worksheet to the new values. Select Cancel or press ESC to return to the worksheet without changing the values.

GRIDLINES

See DISPLAY DEFAULT SETTINGS.

GROUPING AND UNGROUPING OBJECTS

Grouping several graphic objects together allows you to treat them as a single object for ease of sizing, moving, and formatting.

Grouping Objects

To group several objects:

1. Click on the first object. Handles appear around it.

2. Press SHIFT, hold it down, and click on each object you want in the group. Handles appear around each object. You can now format, size, and move the objects together as a single object.

Ungrouping Objects

Grouped objects will need to be separated at some point so that they can be dealt with individually.

- To ungroup the entire group of objects, click anywhere on the worksheet.

- To ungroup a single object from a group, press SHIFT and click on the desired object. The handles disappear around the selected object, but they remain around the rest of the grouped objects.

Note *If you click the Drawing Selection button on the Drawing toolbar, you can limit all selecting to objects (no cells); prevent running a macro that may be attached to an object; and select a group of objects by first dragging a box around the objects to be selected.*

HEADERS

See FORMATTING A DOCUMENT, "Header/Footer Options," for information on headers.

HELP

Excel provides an extensive Help system that gives you a basic description of Excel features and the procedures for using the features.

Basics for Using Help

This section describes how to display a table of Help contents and navigate around the Help system.

1. Select Help | Contents or press F1. The Microsoft Excel Help window appears with a list of topics.

2. Click on the topic you need help with, or press TAB or SHIFT-TAB to move through the list and press ENTER to select the help topic.

3. Select the Search button to display the Search dialog box. Follow the instructions for locating features not found on the contents list.

4. Select the Back button to return to the previously displayed Help screen.

5. Select the History button to display a list of all the Help features looked at during the current Help session.

6. Select the Index button to display a complete index of all the features for which help is provided. Click on a letter button or press TAB or SHIFT-TAB to highlight a button and then press ENTER to display help items beginning with that letter. (You can also display the index by selecting Help | Index from the main menu bar.)

7. Select File | Exit to close the Help window.

Searching for a Specific Help Topic

This feature is useful when you need help with a specific topic and you're not sure how the information is catalogued.

1. Select Help | Search. The Search dialog box appears.

2. Type in a word that pertains to the type of help you want, or select a word from the displayed list of topics.

3. Select Show Topics to display a list of topics in the list box at the bottom of the dialog box.

4. Select a topic and select Go To to display the help information for that topic.

Introducing the Basics of Excel

The Excel tutorial program explains the basics of Excel, describes the latest features, shows you how to get additional information while working with Excel, and provides help for users of Lotus 1-2-3.

1. Select Help | Quick Preview to start the program.

2. Select the topic you are interested in and follow the instructions on the screen.

3. Select Close to end the tutorial at any time.

Learning to Use Excel

There is a series of tutorials designed to show you how to work with databases, worksheets, macros, charts, toolbars, and much more.

1. Select Help | Examples and Demos to display a table of contents for each tutorial.

2. Select the topic that interests you and follow the instructions for the tutorial.

3. Select Close to end the tutorial at any time.

Transitioning from Lotus 1-2-3 to Excel

If you are transitioning from Lotus 1-2-3 to Excel, this Help feature will show you the equivalent Excel commands.

1. Select Help | Lotus 1-2-3 to display the Help for Lotus 1-2-3 Users dialog box.

2. Select from the Menu list box the Lotus menu command you want help with.

3. Select Instructions to display written instructions on the screen, or Demo to run a visual demonstration of the selected feature.

4. Change the pace of the demonstration by selecting Faster or Slower to display a number between 1 and 5, 1 being the slowest speed and 5 the fastest.

5. Select OK or press ENTER.

Multiplan Command Equivalents in Excel

Use this help feature when you need the Excel equivalent of a Multiplan command.

1. Select Help | Multiplan to display the Multiplan Help dialog box.

2. Type the Multiplan command in the Command box.

3. Select OK or press ENTER.

Obtaining Product Support

Provides answers for commonly asked questions about Excel and information on support services in the United States and worldwide.

1. Select Help | Technical Support to display the Excel Technical Support window.
2. Select the help topic from the list and follow the instructions on the screen.

Information About Excel and Your System

Display information about your Excel program and computer system including the program version, registration, serial number, available memory, and hardware resources.

1. Select Help | About Microsoft Excel to display the About Microsoft Excel dialog box.
2. Select System Info. The Microsoft System Info dialog box appears.
3. You can select various system categories from the Choose a Category drop-down list.
4. Select Run to run one of several Windows programs.
5. Select Print to print a copy of each system category.
6. Select Save to save your system information into a file named MSINFO.TXT in the Windows directory.
7. Select Close to exit the Microsoft System Info dialog box.

HIDING AND UNHIDING A WORKBOOK

See WINDOWING TECHNIQUES, "Hiding and Unhiding a Workbook Window."

HIDING AND UNHIDING A WORKSHEET

It is easy to hide a worksheet from view. However, there must be two or more worksheets in a workbook before you can hide a worksheet.

Hiding a Worksheet

To hide a worksheet within a workbook:

1. Select the worksheet to be hidden.
2. Select Format | Sheet | Hide.

Note *The worksheet is only hidden from view, not deleted from the disk or from the workbook. When the workbook is saved, the hidden worksheet is also saved.*

Unhiding a Worksheet

To unhide a worksheet:

1. Select Format | Sheet | Unhide. The Unhide dialog box appears with the currently hidden worksheets listed in the Unhide Sheet list box.
2. Select the worksheet to be unhidden.
3. Select OK or press ENTER.

INSERTING CELLS, ROWS, AND COLUMNS

Insert a blank cell or range of cells, including rows and columns, within a worksheet. Existing cells, rows, or columns will be pushed to the right or down to make room for the inserted cells.

Note *Formulas that move are automatically revised to correspond to their new location.*

Inserting Cells

To insert cells into a worksheet:

1. Determine the location and size of the area to be inserted and then select that area.

2. Select Insert | Cells; click the right mouse button and select Insert; or press CTRL and hold it down while pressing the + key on the numeric keypad. The Insert dialog box is displayed.

3. Specify where you want the existing data to move. You can also insert an entire row or column.

4. Select OK or press ENTER to insert the blank cells.

Inserting Columns and Rows

To insert a column or row into a worksheet:

1. Select one or more rows or columns by clicking on the row or column headings. The new columns or rows will be inserted into the selected area, pushing any data in that area to the right or down.

2. Select Insert | Columns or Insert | Rows, or click the right mouse button and select Insert. The columns or rows are immediately inserted. Existing data in the selected columns or rows shifts to the right or down.

Note *To insert a row or column from the keyboard, press CTRL and hold it down while pressing the + key on the numeric keypad. Then select Entire Row or Entire Column from the Insert dialog box and press ENTER. If you have selected an entire row or column, the new row or column is automatically inserted without the dialog box appearing.*

INSERTING DATA FROM THE CLIPBOARD

Insert data saved to the Clipboard into a document. Surrounding data will shift right or down. This command is different from Edit | Paste.

1. Place data into the Clipboard with the Edit | Copy or Edit | Cut commands.
2. Select the cell, row, or column in which the cut or copied data will appear.
3. Select Insert | Copied Cells, or click the right mouse button on the selected cell and select Insert Copied Cells. The Insert Paste dialog box appears.
4. Select the direction you want existing data to shift.
5. Select OK or press ENTER to insert the text.

INSERTING OBJECTS FROM OTHER APPLICATIONS

Inserting a New Object

To create and insert, or embed, an object into a worksheet:

1. Determine an area of the worksheet where you want the object to appear and select a cell.
2. Select Insert | Object. The Object dialog box appears.
3. Select the Create New tab.
4. Select the type of object from the Object Type list box.
5. Check the Display as Icon box if you want the embedded object to appear as an icon on the worksheet. Some objects always appear as icons.
6. Select OK or press ENTER to run the application associated with the chart object.

7. Create the object. When finished, select File | Update from the application menu bar. The object is placed into the Excel worksheet.

8. Exit the object application and return to the Excel worksheet. Should you at any time wish to edit the inserted object, double-click on the object to start the associated application, make the edits, and exit the application.

Inserting an Existing File

To insert, or embed, an entire file into a worksheet:

1. Determine an area of the worksheet where you want the embedded file to appear and select a cell.

2. Select Insert | Object. The Object dialog box appears.

3. Select the Create from File tab.

4. Check the Display as Icon box to have the file display as an icon on the worksheet.

5. Check the Link to File box to establish a link with the embedded object and the source object. When the source object is edited, the embedded object will reflect those edits.

6. Locate and highlight the filename.

7. Select OK or press ENTER to insert the file into the worksheet.

INSERTING PICTURES

To insert a graphic into a worksheet from a variety of different graphics file formats:

1. Select Insert | Picture. The Picture dialog box appears.

2. Select the directory where the desired graphic files are stored. If you have difficulty finding the graphic file you want, select Find File to do a file search.

3. Select the type of file formats you want to choose from by dropping down the List Files of Type list.

4. Select the desired graphic file from the File <u>N</u>ame list box.
5. Check the <u>P</u>review Picture check box to view the graphic before inserting it in your document.
6. Select OK to insert the graphic into the worksheet.

JUSTIFYING TEXT

To convert a column of text into a word-wrapped paragraph:

1. Select the column of text. The text must be in the left-most column and blank cells in the rest of the range.
2. Select <u>E</u>dit | Fi<u>l</u>l | <u>J</u>ustify. The text is wrapped within the selected range of cells.

Note *If the wrapped text extends below the last row in the selected range, you will see a dialog box warning you that the range is not large enough to accommodate the data. Select OK or press ENTER to continue, or select Cancel to stop the operation. This prevents overwriting important data below the selected range.*

LINKING DOCUMENTS

Linking Workbooks and Worksheets

Link cells in a workbook or worksheet to source data in the same workbook or worksheet or another workbook or worksheet. When the source data is changed, the linked data will automatically be updated to reflect that change.

1. Select the range of cells in the source worksheet and use the <u>E</u>dit | <u>C</u>opy command to move the data into the Clipboard.

2. Switch to the workbook or worksheet to be linked (can be the same worksheet) and select a range of cells the same size as the range that was copied into the Clipboard.

3. Select Edit | Paste Special to display the Paste Special dialog box. To paste a link into more than one workbook or worksheet, repeat steps 2 and 3 for each link.

4. Select Paste Link. The source data is pasted into the workbook or worksheet. Whenever you change the source data, the pasted data will be updated to reflect the change.

Note *When you open a workbook containing worksheets that contain links to another source, you will be asked if you want to update the links. Select Yes if you want the linked worksheets to reflect any changes made in the source worksheets.*

Linking Excel with Other Applications

To link an Excel document to a document in another application, or to link a document from another application to an Excel document:

1. Start Excel and the other application.

2. Switch to the source document in either Excel or the other application.

3. Select the source data you want to link to the other application and copy it into the Clipboard using the Edit | Copy command.

4. Switch to the other document and select the location where the source data is to be pasted.

5. For pasting data into an application other than Excel, follow that applications procedures for pasting linked data into a document. If you are pasting source data into Excel, select Edit | Paste Special. The Paste Special dialog box appears.

6. Select Paste Link. If the Paste Link radio button is not available, the other application is not capable of providing the data in a usable format.

7. In the As box, select the type of object you are linking.

8. Select Display as Icon to display the object as an icon with a title. You can also change the icon, if icons are available.

9. Select OK or press ENTER to insert the object into the Excel worksheet. Double-clicking on the object will start the associated application and display the linked file.

Editing Links

To edit source documents linked to the active document:

1. You must have opened a document that contains links to source documents.

2. Select Edit | Links. The Links dialog box appears with a list of source files in the Source File list box.

3. Select the source files to be edited. (Press the DOWN ARROW key to highlight the filename.)

4. Select Open to open the source files. You can then make edits to the source data.

Options

Close/Cancel
The Close button cancels the command and closes the Links dialog box. The Cancel button appears after some action is taken in the dialog box. Select Cancel to reverse the action and close the dialog box.

Update Now
Updates the active worksheet to reflect any changes made to the selected source files.

Change Source
See "Changing the Source File."

Automatic
Automatically updates linked data.

Manual
Manually updates linked data when the Update Now button is selected.

Changing the Source File

Replace the selected source file with another file of your choosing. The linked cells on the active worksheet will be updated to reflect the source cells on the newly selected source file.

1. Open a document that is linked to source documents.
2. Select Edit | Links to display the Links dialog box.
3. Select the source file to be changed and select Change Source. The Change Links dialog box appears.
4. Select the name of the file that will become the new source worksheet or type the filename in the File Name box.
5. Select OK or press ENTER.

MOVING AND COPYING WORKSHEETS

Move or copy one or more worksheets to another place in the same workbook or to another workbook.

1. Select the tabs of the worksheets to be moved.
2. To move the worksheets, click on the worksheet tabs and drag them to a new location along the line of tabs at the bottom of the screen. You can also drag the worksheets into another open workbook.
3. To copy the worksheets, press CTRL and hold it down while you drag the worksheet tabs to another location in the same workbook or into another open workbook.

Note *To move or copy the selected worksheets using the menu system, select Edit | Move or Copy Sheet to display the Move or Copy dialog box.*

4. To move the worksheet to another workbook, select another open workbook from the To Book drop-down list.

5. To move a worksheet in the same workbook, select the destination worksheet in the Before Sheet box. The moved worksheet will be placed before the selected worksheet.

6. To copy the worksheets, check the Create a Sheet box.

NAMES

A name represents a cell, a range of cells, a formula, or a value, allowing those items to be referred to by name rather than cell references. This section describes how to define and apply a name, create several names at the same time from text that appears in a selected range of cells, edit an existing name, and delete a name.

Defining a Name

To define a name:

1. If creating a new name, first select the range to be named.

2. Select Insert | Name | Define to display the Define Name dialog box. Notice that the reference for the currently selected cells appears in the Refers to box.

3. To assign a name for the selected range, type the name in the Names in Workbook box.

4. To specify a new reference, select the Refers to box and type in the new reference range, or click on the worksheet and select the reference range with the mouse.

5. Select Add to add the range name to the list.

Using the Name Box

Create or edit a name in the name box located at the far left end of the formula bar. Clicking on the down-arrow displays a list of existing names.

1. Select the range to be named and click in the name box. If a cell or range has a name already, the name will appear in the name box.

2. Type in a name and press ENTER.

3. To edit an existing name, click on the arrow on the formula bar to display a drop-down list with the existing names.

4. Click on a name to display it in the name box.

5. Edit the name and press ENTER.

Note *If you are creating a formula and the formula bar is active, select a name from the name box drop-down list to insert the name into the formula.*

Creating Several Names

To create several names at the same time:

1. Enter the names to be created in a column or row adjacent to their respective ranges.

2. Select a range of cells to be named and include the names you just entered on the left, right, top, or bottom edge of the selected range.

3. Select Insert | Name | Create, or press CTRL-SHIFT-F3. The Create Names dialog box appears.

4. Select the check boxes that describe the location of the names in the selected range.

5. Select OK or press ENTER.

Editing an Existing Name

To edit an existing name:

1. Select Edit | Name | Define, or press CTRL-F3 to display the Define Name dialog box.

2. Select the name to be edited from the list box. The name appears in the Names in Workbook box.

3. To change the name, select Names in Workbook and edit the name.

4. Select Refers to, delete the current reference, and then type in a new reference or select it directly on the worksheet.

5. Select OK or press ENTER when you are finished.

Deleting a Name

To delete a name:

1. Select Insert I Name I Define to display the Define Name dialog box.

2. Select the name to be deleted from the Names in Workbook list box.

3. Select Delete. The name is removed from the list.

Note *Be careful! A deleted name cannot be undone.*

Replacing a Formula Cell-Reference with an Existing Name

Search through formulas in a selection and substitute a name in place of a formula cell reference. This command works in conjunction with Insert I Name I Create and Insert I Name I Define.

1. Select the cell or cells that contain the formulas to be searched.

2. Select Insert I Name I Apply. The Apply Names dialog box appears with a list of the currently defined names for the active worksheet.

3. Select the names that represent the cell references. To select (or deselect) more than one name, press and hold down the CTRL button, and then press SPACEBAR or click on the name.

4. Select OK or press ENTER. The formula cell references will now have names instead of cell references.

Options

Ignore Relative/Absolute
Turn on to replace a cell reference with a name regardless of the reference type.

Use Row and Column Names

Turn on to replace a cell reference with the names of row and column ranges containing the cells referred to when an exact match is not found.

Options Button

Omit Column Name if Same Column

Turn on to use a row-oriented name even though a column-oriented name is assigned to the same cell.

Omit Row Name if Same Row

Turn on to use a column-oriented name range even though a row-oriented name range is assigned to the same cell.

Name Order

Determines which name will appear first in both a row-oriented and column-oriented name range.

NAMING A WORKSHEET IN A WORKBOOK

To assign a name to a worksheet:

1. Select the worksheet to be named.
2. Select Format | Sheet | Rename. The Rename Sheet dialog box appears.
3. Select Name and type a name for the worksheet.
4. Select OK or press ENTER. The name will appear on the worksheet tab.

Note   *A name can have up to 31 characters. You can include spaces, but none of the following characters: square brackets, colon, slash mark, backslash, question mark, or asterisk.*

NOTES IN CELLS

Create and work with cell notes. A cell note does not
appear on the worksheet, but can be printed with the
worksheet if you choose. You can also edit, view, add, or
delete notes in a cell.

Adding a Note

To add a note to a cell:

1. Select a cell in which you want to place a note.
2. Select Insert | Note; click on the Attach Note button on
   the Auditing toolbar; or press SHIFT-F2 to display the Cell
   Note dialog box. Existing notes appear in the Notes in
   Sheet box.
3. Select Text Note and type a new note.
4. Select Add to add the note to the list in the Notes in
   Sheet box.
5. If you want to add an additional note to another cell,
   select Cell, type in a new cell address, and repeat steps
   3 and 4.
6. Select OK or press ENTER to return to the worksheet. A
   small block appears in the upper-right corner of a cell
   that contains a note.

Deleting a Note

To delete a note from a cell:

1. Select Insert | Note; click on the Attach Note button on
   the Auditing toolbar; or press SHIFT-F2. The Cell Note
   dialog box appears.
2. Select the note to be deleted from the Notes in Sheet box.
3. Select Delete. You are alerted that the note will be
   permanently deleted. Undo will not recover a deleted note.
4. Select OK or press ENTER to return to the worksheet.

Viewing and Editing a Note

To view and edit a note in a cell:

1. Select Insert | Note, or click on the Attach Note button on the Auditing toolbar, or press SHIFT-F2 to display the Cell Note dialog box.

2. Select the note to be viewed and edited from the Notes in Sheet box. The text of the note appears in the Text Note box.

3. Select Text Note and make the appropriate edits.

4. Select Add to place the edited note back on the Notes on Sheet list.

5. Select OK or press ENTER to return to the worksheet.

NUMBERS, DATES, AND TIME VALUES

Modifying the Appearance of Numbers, Dates, and Time Values

Modify how numbers, dates, and time values are displayed on the screen. Excel allows you to use built-in number formats, or you can create your own customized format.

1. Select the range of cells that contain the numerical data. The numerical data can include numbers, dates, or time values.

2. Select Format | Cells; click the right mouse button on the selected range and select Format Cells; or press CTRL-1. The Format Cells dialog box appears.

3. Select the Number tab to display the number options.

4. Select the appropriate formatting option from the Category list. The format codes for that category appear in the Format Codes list box.

5. Select Format Codes and choose a format from the list.

6. To customize a format, select Code and type in a custom format.

7. Select OK or press ENTER.

OBJECTS IN WORKSHEETS

Attaching Objects to Cells

You may position graphic objects by attaching them to cells. You can also specify how the objects will move and change size relative to the cells underlying the object.

1. Select the object to be moved or sized.

2. Select Format | Object; click the right mouse button on the object and select Format Object; or press CTRL-1 to display the Format Object dialog box.

3. Select the Properties tab and select the desired object placement options (*see* "Placement Options").

4. Unselect the Print Object check box to prevent the object from printing.

5. Select OK or press ENTER.

Placement Options

Move and Size with Cells
The object will change position and size itself with the cells under the object's upper-left and lower-right corners.

Move but Don't Size with Cells
The object will move with the cells under its upper-left corner, but the object will not change size.

Don't Move or Size with Cells
The object remains in its current location and maintains the same size regardless of how the underlying cells change.

Note   *The Cut and Copy commands affect the contents of a cell but not the cell itself; therefore, an object will not move or size when these commands are used. Imported pictures will move, but not change size with the cells.*

Bringing an Object to the Front

To move an object in front of all other objects in the worksheet:

1. Select a graphic object in the background that you want to place in front of other objects.

2. Select Format | Placement | Bring to Front, or click the right mouse button on the object and select Bring to Front. The selected object moves in front of the other objects.

Sending an Object to the Back

To move an object to the rear of all other objects in the worksheet:

1. Select the object.

2. Select Format | Placement | Send to Back, or click the right mouse button on the object and select Send to Back. The selected object moves behind the other objects.

OPENING WORKBOOKS

Opening an Existing Workbook

To open a document that has been saved and is no longer on the screen:

1. Select File | Open; click on the Open File button on the Standard toolbar; or press CTRL-O. The Open dialog box is displayed.

2. Select the disk drive where the file is located from the Drives drop-down list.

3. Select the directory where the file is stored from the Directories list box.

4. Select the desired file from the list of files displayed in the File Name list box. (You can restrict the types of files displayed by selecting a file type from the List Files of Type drop-down list box.)

5. Select the Read Only check box to view the file without making any changes.

6. Select OK or press ENTER to open the file.

Note *See FILE MANAGEMENT for a description of the Find File option.*

Opening a New Workbook

To start a new workbook:

1. Select File | New, or click on the New Workbook button on the Standard toolbar. The new workbook appears in the application window.

Opening a Recently Opened Workbook

Excel remembers the four most recently opened workbooks. To open them directly from the File pull-down menu:

1. Select File. The pull-down menu appears. The filenames of the four most recently opened files appear near the bottom of the pull-down menu.

2. Select the file you want to open.

OPERATORS AND ORDER OF PRECEDENCE

Calculations done in Excel are based on two things: operators and order of precedence. An *operator* specifies a function to be carried out during the evaluation of a formula. Operators can be arithmetic, text, comparison, or reference types. The *order of precedence* determines the order in which operators are evaluated. Order of precedence is sometimes referred to as order of *evaluation* or *calculation*.

The following list gives the order in which operators are calculated during the evaluation of a formula.

Operator	Type	Function (Order of Precedence)
:	Reference	Evaluate the range of cells (1)
A space	Reference	Evaluate the intersection of cells (2)
,	Reference	Evaluates to one reference that includes two references (3)
– (minus)	Arithmetic	Negation (4)
%	Arithmetic	Percentage (5)
^	Arithmetic	Exponentiation (6)
*	Arithmetic	Multiplication (7)
/	Arithmetic	Division (7)
+	Arithmetic	Addition (8)
– (minus)	Arithmetic	Subtraction (8)
&	Text	Concatenates (connects) to text values (9)
=	Comparison	Equal to (10)
<	Comparison	Less than (10)
<=	Comparison	Less than or equal to (10)
>	Comparison	Greater than (10)
>=	Comparison	Greater than or equal to (10)
<>	Comparison	Not equal to (10)

Note *The lower the precedence number, the sooner the operator is evaluated. Operators with the same order of precedence are evaluated from left to right as they appear in the formula. To change the order of precedence in a formula, enclose the values and operators in parentheses. The formula in the innermost set of parentheses will be calculated first.*

OUTLINING WORKSHEET DATA

Create an outline for the purpose of creating a summary report. An outline can have no more than eight levels of vertical or horizontal groups.

Note *You can create only a single outline for each worksheet.*

Creating an Outline Automatically

To automatically create an outline of your data:

1. Select the range of cells to be included in the outline. Selecting a single cell will result in the entire worksheet being outlined.

2. Select Data | Group and Outline | Auto Outline. The data is outlined.

Creating an Outline Manually

To manually create an outline:

1. Select either a group of rows or a group of columns.

2. Select Data | Group and Outline | Group. The selected rows or columns are now in a group and can be hidden or shown as desired.

Clearing an Outline

To clear an outline from the worksheet:

1. Select the columns or rows to be removed from the outline.

2. Select Data | Group and Outline | Clear Outline. The outline is cleared, but the data is unchanged.

Showing and Hiding Outline Details

The appearance of an outline can be altered by showing and hiding details in an outline group. If you use a mouse, you can even show specific levels of an outline by hiding or showing outline details.

Hiding Outline Details

1. Select the entire outline range, or, if a group is to be hidden, select a cell containing the summary data in that group.

2. Select Data | Group and Outline | Hide Details. The details of the entire outline or the selected group disappear from the screen, but the hidden cells are not deleted from the worksheet.

Showing Outline Details

1. Select all or a portion of the outline where details are hidden.

2. Select Data | Group and Outline | Show Details. The hidden details appear in the outline.

Establishing Outline Settings

To set the outline options that are applied when creating an outline:

1. Select Data | Group and Outline | Settings to display the Outline dialog box.

2. Select one or both of the options in the Direction box to specify where the summary rows and columns are located.

3. Check the Automatic Styles box to automatically apply built-in cell styles for the summary rows and columns.

4. Select Create to automatically assign outline levels based on the formulas in your worksheet. If the Automatic Styles check box is checked, the built-in cell styles are applied.

5. Select Apply Styles to apply rows and column level styles to the entire outline or to selected portions of it.

PAGE BREAKS

This feature lets you manually set or remove page breaks in a worksheet.

Setting a Page Break

To set a page break:

1. Select a cell located below and to the right of where the page break should appear.
2. Select Insert | Page Break to insert the page break.

Removing a Page Break

To remove a page break:

1. Select a cell directly below or to the right of the page break to be removed.
2. Select Options | Remove Page Break. (The Remove Page Break command will only appear on the pull-down menu if the selected cell is next to the page break.)

PAGE NUMBERING

See FORMATTING A DOCUMENT, "Page Options."

PARSING IMPORTED DATA

Import data from another program either by retrieving a file or by copying and pasting through the Clipboard. You may want the imported data to be distributed across several columns. Sometimes data is imported into a single worksheet cell and needs to be parsed, or separated, into several cells.

1. Import the data into an Excel worksheet. If you import the worksheet data through the Clipboard, complete steps 2 through 7.

   If you import a file, the Text Import Wizard dialog box opens. You can skip steps 2 and 3 and go to the Text Wizard instructions in steps 4 through 8 to specify how the data will be entered on the worksheet.

2. Select the cells that contain the imported data. You can only select data in one column, but in any number of rows in that column.

3. Select Data | Text to Columns. The first of three Convert Text to Columns Wizard dialog boxes appears. The data to be parsed appears in the Preview window.

4. Select Delimited or Fixed Width, depending on the type of data you've imported. For an imported file you can also specify the file origin and the row where the imported text will begin on the worksheet.

5. Select Next to move to the second Text Wizard dialog box. If you selected Fixed Width, line breaks may or may not separate the text. Follow the instructions on the screen for adding, deleting, or modifying the line breaks. If you selected Delimited, select the delimiters you need. Line breaks appear at the delimiter locations.

6. Select Next to display the third Text Wizard dialog box.

7. Specify the data format for the text. If your data is separated by line breaks, you can select each column and specify a data format. The formats available are General, Text, Date, and Do Not Import Column (Skip). To parse the data into another location, select Destination and type the cell reference for the left-most cell in which the data will appear.

8. Select Finish to parse the data into the worksheet.

PASTING DATA

Pasting Clipboard Data as a Graphic

See COPYING A PICTORIAL REPRESENTATION.

Pasting Data from the Clipboard

See CUTTING AND PASTING DATA.

PASTING A PICTURE LINKED TO THE SOURCE DATA

Paste a picture that is linked with the source data. When source data is changed, the picture is updated to reflect that change. You can paste a picture link in the same worksheet, in another worksheet, or in another workbook.

1. Select the range of cells to be pasted as a picture and use the Edit | Copy command, or click on the Copy button on the Standard toolbar to copy the selection to the Clipboard.

2. Select the worksheet or workbook and then select the area of the worksheet where the picture will appear.

3. Press SHIFT, hold it down, and select Edit | Paste Picture Link. A picture of the selected data is pasted into the worksheet.

PASTING SELECTED ATTRIBUTES

You can paste specific attributes from pasted data. This feature allows you to combine data to be pasted with data that exists in the cells where the pasted data will appear.

1. Select the range of cells to be pasted and use the Edit | Copy command, or click on the Copy button on the Standard toolbar to copy the selection to the Clipboard.

2. Select the area of the worksheet where the copied data will appear.

3. Select Edit | Paste Special to display the Paste Special dialog box.

4. Select the appropriate Paste option (*see* "Paste Options") to select the attributes of the copied data that you want to paste into the destination cells.

5. Select the appropriate Operation option (*see* "Operations Options").

6. Select Skip Blanks to avoid copying blank cells from the Clipboard.

7. Select Transpose to transpose a column of data into rows or to transpose rows of data into columns.

8. Select OK or press ENTER.

Note   *If a group of worksheets is selected, Paste Special pastes properties of the copied cells into the corresponding paste area on each sheet in the selected group.*

Paste Options

All
Pastes all cell attributes into the paste area.

Formulas
Pastes only formulas as entered in the formula bar.

Values
Pastes only displayed cell values.

Formats
Pastes only cell formats.

Notes
Pastes only cell notes.

Operations Options

None
Replaces the destination data with the copied data.

Add
Adds the copied formulas or values to those located in the destination cells.

Subtract
Subtracts the copied data from the data located in the destination cells.

Multiply
Multiplies the copied data by the data in the destination area.

Divide
Divides the copied data into the data located in the destination area.

Paste Link
Pastes copied data into selected cells and links the data with the source data.

When the source data changes, the copied data reflects those changes.

Paste Special Dialog Box Options When an Object is Selected

As
Lists the forms in which the data can be pasted.

Paste
Pastes the data stored in the Clipboard into the worksheet.

Paste Link
Links the pasted data to its source data. If a link cannot be established, this button will be grayed out.

Display As Icon
Displays the pasted object as an icon that represents the source application.

PRINTING

Previewing a Document

To view and make minor formatting changes to a document prior to printing:

1. Display the document to be printed.
2. Select File | Print Preview to display the preview screen.
3. Select Close to return to the document.

Print Preview Options

Next/Previous
Display the next or previous page of the document.

Zoom
Switch between the full screen size and the full page size.

Print
Display the Print dialog box and print the worksheet. (*See* "Printing a Document" for more information.)

Setup
Display the Page Setup dialog box. (*See* FORMATTING A DOCUMENT for more information.)

Margins
Change the worksheet margins, header and footer margins, and column widths by dragging the black handles to the desired locations.

Printing a Document

To select various options to prepare a document for printing:

1. Display the document to be printed. (If you do not want to print the entire worksheet, *see* "Printing a Portion of a Worksheet.")
2. Select File | Print; click on the Print button on the Standard toolbar; or press CTRL-P. The Print dialog box appears.
3. Select the desired print options (see "Print Options").
4. Select OK or press ENTER to print the document.

Note   *To bypass the menu selections and immediately print a worksheet, click on the Print button on the Standard toolbar.*

Print Options

Print What
Print either a Selection from the worksheet, Selected Sheet(s), or the Entire Workbook.

Copies
Type the number, or click on the up or down arrow to designate the number of copies to be printed.

Page Range
Select All to print every page. Select Pages and type the desired page numbers in the From and To boxes.

Page Setup
Display the Page Setup dialog box and format the page output. (*See* FORMATTING A DOCUMENT for more information.)

Print Preview
View the document before it prints.

Printer Setup

Display a list of printers from which to choose for printing the document.

Printing a Portion of a Worksheet

You can choose between two methods for printing a selected area of a worksheet.

Method One

1. Select the range to be printed and then select File | Print. The Print dialog box appears.
2. Select Selection.
3. Select OK or press ENTER to print the selected range.

Method Two

1. Select File | Print to display the Print dialog box.
2. Select Page Setup. The Page Setup dialog box appears.
3. Select Print Area and type in the print range, or select the range directly off the worksheet by dragging the mouse over the desired area.
4. Click on OK or press ENTER to accept the range.
5. Select Selected Sheet(s) and click on OK or press ENTER to print the range.

Setting Print Titles

To set or remove print titles that appear on every page of the document:

See FORMATTING A DOCUMENT, "Sheet Options."

Scaling Printed Data to Fit the Page

To reduce or enlarge the size of the printed data so the data will fit on more or fewer pages:

See FORMATTING A DOCUMENT, "Page Options."

PROTECTING WORKBOOKS AND WORKSHEETS

Prevent documents from being viewed or edited by others. You can protect a workbook, a worksheet, a range of cells, or an object. You can assign a password that is case sensitive, limited to 15 characters, and composed of numbers, letters, and symbols.

Note *Do not forget your password; you cannot access the locked information without it. Store a copy of all passwords in a secure place.*

Editing Cells and Objects in a Locked Worksheet

This feature allows a specified range of cells and selected objects to remain unlocked while the rest of the worksheet is protected. This allows the unlocked cells or objects to be edited at any time.

1. Display the worksheet to be protected.

2. Select the range of cells or objects that is to be unprotected.

3. Select Format | Cells/Object; click the right mouse button and select Format Cells/Object; or press CTRL-1. The Format Cells or Format Object dialog box appears.

4. Select the Protection tab and clear the check from the Locked or Lock Text check box. Only the selected cells or objects are unlocked.

5. Select OK or press ENTER to return to the worksheet.

For information on protecting the worksheet, see "Activating Cell Protection."

Protecting an Object or Text Box

Prevent an object or text box from being moved or changed. Objects and text boxes must have locking turned on or they will not be protected when the worksheet is protected.

1. Select the objects and text boxes to be protected.

2. Select Format | Object; click the right mouse button and select Format Object; or press CTRL-1. The Format Object dialog box appears.

3. Click on the Protection tab.

4. Place a check in the Locked check box. If the object is a text box, place a check in the Lock Text check box.

5. Select OK or press ENTER.

For information on protecting the worksheet, see "Activating Cell Protection."

Protecting an Open Workbook

Restrict the viewing or editing of an open workbook. You can protect a workbook's window from being tampered with, and you can protect the structure of the worksheets within a workbook.

1. Select Tools | Protection | Protect Workbook to display the Protect Workbook dialog box.

2. Type in a password in the Password box.

3. Place a check in the Structure box to prevent new worksheets from being added or existing worksheets from being moved, hidden or unhidden, deleted, or renamed.

4. Place a check in the Windows box to prevent the workbook windows from being resized, moved, hidden or unhidden, or closed.

5. Select OK or press ENTER to accept the password and options.

6. If you entered a password, you will have to retype it for confirmation and select OK or press ENTER to return to the workbook.

Protecting a Workbook from Being Opened or Saved

To restrict access to a workbook:

1. Select File | Save As to display the Save As dialog box.
2. Select Options. The Save Options dialog box appears.
3. Select the protection option that is appropriate to your security needs (*see* "Save Options").
4. Select OK or press ENTER to return to the Save As dialog box.
5. Assign a filename and select OK or press ENTER.

Save Options

Always Create Backup

A backup copy of a workbook is created each time you save the workbook. A backup copy is the previous version of the workbook and has the same name as the current version with a .BAK extension.

Protection Password

Prevents the workbook from being opened. Type the password, press ENTER, and type the password a second time for confirmation.

Write Reservation Password

Allows the workbook to be edited, but it must be saved with a different filename, thereby preserving the original workbook. Type the password, press ENTER, and type the password a second time for confirmation.

Read–Only Recommended

Alerts the user that the workbook should only be read, not edited. Edits can be made, but the file can only be saved under a different name, thereby preserving the original workbook.

Protecting a Worksheet

Prevent a worksheet from being edited. Before a worksheet can be protected, you must specify that cells will be locked when protection is activated.

1. Display the worksheet to be protected.
2. Select Format | Cells; click the right mouse button and select Format Cells; or press CTRL-1. The Format Cells dialog box appears.
3. Select the Protection tab and select Locked to prevent the cell contents from being edited. Select Hidden so that the formulas will not appear on the formula bar.
4. Select OK or press ENTER. To activate the cell protection, follow the steps in the following section.

Activating Cell Protection

1. Select Tools | Protection | Protect Sheet. The Protect Sheet dialog box appears.
2. Type a password in the Password box. Place a check in the Contents, Objects, and Scenarios boxes to provide specific protection for those items. Remove the check if you don't want to protect a particular item.
3. Select OK or press ENTER.
4. If you typed a password, you will be asked to verify the password. Type the password again and select OK.

Unprotecting a Workbook or a Worksheet

To unprotect a workbook or a worksheet:

1. Display the protected workbook or worksheet.
2. Select Tools | Protection to display the Protection submenu.
3. Select Unprotect Sheet or Unprotect Workbook.
4. If a password has been assigned, type the password in the Password box and select OK or press ENTER.

RENAMING A WORKSHEET

See NAMING A WORKSHEET IN A WORKBOOK.

REPEATING EXCEL OPERATIONS

To repeat the most recent operation made from a menu or dialog box:

1. Perform an operation from a menu or dialog box.
2. Move to the new location where you want to repeat the same operation.
3. Select Edit | Repeat, or press ALT-ENTER or F4. The operation repeats. The name of the operation to be repeated follows the Repeat command on the pull-down menu.

Note *For operations that cannot be repeated, the Edit | Repeat option is grayed out.*

REPLACING EXISTING CHARACTERS

To locate specific data and replace it with different data:

1. Select a range of cells in which you want to search for data. If a range is not selected, the entire worksheet is searched.
2. Select Edit | Replace, or press CTRL-H. The Replace dialog box appears.
3. Select Find What and type the data to be searched for and replaced. Wildcard symbols ? and * can be used.
4. Select Replace With and enter the data that will replace the data entered in the Find What box.

5. Select the search options (*see* "Search Options").

6. Select <u>F</u>ind Next to locate the next occurrence of the search data. Press SHIFT, hold it down, and select <u>F</u>ind Next to search *backward* through the worksheet.

7. Select <u>R</u>eplace to replace the found data, or select Replace <u>A</u>ll to replace each occurrence of the search data without stopping.

8. When all replacements have been made, select Close or press ESC to return to the worksheet.

Note   *Because the search is backward through a worksheet, place the active cell beyond the area you want to search when searching the entire worksheet.*

Search Options

<u>S</u>earch by Rows and Columns
Conduct the search across rows or down columns.

Match <u>C</u>ase
Mark this check box to find search data that matches both uppercase and lowercase characters.

Find Entire Cells <u>O</u>nly
Search for the exact match to the search criteria.

REPORTS

You can create and print a report composed of worksheets, views, or scenarios. A report is useful when you need to print a group of worksheets out of sequence.

Creating and Printing a Report

A report can consist of several sections. Each section must consist of at least a worksheet with an optional view or scenario.

To create and print a report:

1. Select File | Print Report. The Print Report dialog box appears. A list of existing reports appears in the Reports list box. (*See* "Print Report Options.")

2. To create a new report, select Add to display the Add Report dialog box.

3. Type a name for the report in the Report Name box.

4. Select a worksheet from the Sheet drop-down list.

5. If you want to include a view or scenario in the report, check the View or Scenario box desired and select a view or scenario from the appropriate drop-down list.

6. Select Add to add this section of the report.

7. Repeat steps 4 and 5 as many times as necessary to create the needed sections of this report.

8. Check the Use Continuous Page Numbers box to print page numbers on each page of the report.

9. You can rearrange the order of the report sections by selecting the Sections in this Report list box, highlighting a section, and selecting the Move Up or Move Down buttons. Select Delete to delete a highlighted section.

10. Select OK or press ENTER when all the needed sections are added to the report.

11. Select Print or press ENTER to print the report that is highlighted in the Reports list.

Note *The Print Report command will not appear on the File menu unless the Report Manager add-in has been installed and activated. See ADD-INS for instructions on activating an add-in.*

Print Report Options

Reports
Select a report to print, edit, or delete.

Print
Prints the selected report.

Add
Displays the Add dialog box, in which you create reports.

Edit
Displays the Edit dialog box, in which you edit reports.

Delete
Deletes the selected report.

Editing and Deleting a Report

To edit and delete a report:

1. Select File | Print Report to display the Print Report dialog box.

2. To edit a report, highlight the report name in the Reports list box and select Edit. The Edit Report dialog box appears.

3. Make the appropriate edits and select OK or press ENTER to return to the Print Report dialog box. You can then print the report if desired.

4. To delete a report, highlight the report name in the Reports list box and select Delete. You are asked if you want to delete the report.

5. Select OK or press ENTER to delete the report from the list.

6. After you have completed editing or deleting reports, select Close to return to the worksheet.

ROWS

Hiding, Unhiding, and Changing the Height of Rows

This feature hides and unhides or changes the height of selected rows. You cannot use this feature on a protected worksheet.

Hiding Rows

To hide rows:

1. Select at least one cell in each row that you want to hide.
2. Select Format | Row to display the Row submenu.
3. Select Hide to set the height of the selected rows to zero, causing the rows to disappear from the worksheet.

Unhiding Rows

To unhide hidden rows:

1. Select cells from the adjacent rows on each side of the hidden rows, and then select Format | Unhide.

Changing the Height of Rows to Their Standard Size

To adjust the height of each row to its standard height (which is dependent on the size of the largest font):

1. Select at least one cell in each row for which you want to change the height. If you want to change the row height in more than one worksheet at the same time, select each worksheet first (*see* SELECTING, "Selecting Two or More Worksheets in a Workbook").
2. Select AutoFit.

Note   *A shortcut method for expanding a row for the best fit is to double-click on the bottom border of the row heading; for several selected rows, double-click on any border of the row headings.*

Changing the Height of Rows to a Specific Height

To change the height of rows to a specific height:

1. Select at least one cell in each row for which you want to change the height. If you want to change the row height in more than one worksheet at the same time, select each worksheet first (*see* SELECTING, "Selecting Two or More Worksheets in a Workbook").

2. Select H_eight. The Row Height dialog box appears. The standard height of a row depends on the default font.

3. In the _Row Height box, type in a desired height between 0 and 409 points. Entering a zero will hide the rows. Enter decimal fractions for more exact heights.

4. Select OK or press ENTER.

Note   *You can bypass the menu selections and change a row height with the mouse by placing the mouse pointer on the bottom border of the row heading. The pointer turns into a two-headed arrow that you can drag to the desired row height.*

Deleting a Row

See DELETING CELLS, COLUMNS, AND ROWS.

SAVING

Saving and Retrieving Your Workspace

Save the size and screen position of the currently open workbooks. When you retrieve the saved workspace file, the workbooks will be the same size and in the same location as they were when you saved the workspace. This feature lets you pick up work exactly where you left off.

Saving the Workspace

To save the workspace:

1. Select _File | Save _Workspace. The Save Workspace dialog box appears.

2. Select File _Name and enter the new filename.

Workspace files are automatically assigned an .XLW file extension.

3. Select Directories and Drives to specify where the file will be stored, if other than in the displayed drive and directory.

4. Select OK or press ENTER to save the file.

Retrieving the Workspace

To retrieve the workspace:

1. Select File | Open; click on the Open button on the Standard toolbar; or press CTRL-O. The Open dialog box appears.

2. Select the workspace file from the File Name list box.

3. Select OK or press ENTER to open the workspace.

Saving a Workbook

To save the active workbook:

1. Select File | Save; click on the Save button on the Standard toolbar; or press CTRL+S. Your document is immediately saved. If the workbook doesn't have a filename, the Save As dialog box appears.

2. Type a filename in the File Name box.

3. Select the drive and directory where the file will be stored from the Directories and Drives list boxes.

4. Select OK or press ENTER to save the file.

Saving a Workbook with a New Name

To save a previously saved workbook under another filename:

1. Select File | Save As or press F12. The Save As dialog box appears.

2. Select File Name and enter the new filename.

3. Select Directories and Drives to specify where the file will be stored, if other than in the displayed drive and directory.

4. Display the Save File as Type drop-down list and select the type of file format in which you want to save the file.

5. Select the Options button to save the file with a password, to create a backup file, or to designate a file for read-only. (For details, *see* PROTECTING WORKBOOKS AND WORKSHEETS, "Protecting a Workbook from Being Opened or Saved.")

6. Select OK or press ENTER to save the file.

Note   *The original file remains intact on the disk.*

SCENARIO MANAGER

Analyze worksheet data by creating and saving *scenarios*. A scenario consists of different input values that are substituted into a worksheet *model*. A worksheet model is a set of worksheets designed to solve a problem.

Creating, Editing, and Applying a Scenario

To create, edit, and apply a scenario:

1. Open the desired worksheet model, usually located in the EXAMPLES directory. Any worksheet can serve as a model, however.

2. Select Tools | Scenarios to display the Scenario Manager dialog box.

3. Select Add to display the Add Scenario dialog box.

4. Enter a name for the scenario in the Scenario Name box.

5. Select Changing Cells and enter the cell references or names for the cells you want to change. You can also select the changing cells by dragging the mouse over the cells on the worksheet.

6. Select the desired Add Scenario options (*see* "Add Scenario Options") and select OK when finished. The Scenario Values dialog box appears.

7. Enter the values for the changing cells. Select Add to create additional scenarios, if needed, and repeat steps 4 through 7.

8. When finished creating scenarios, select OK to display the Scenario Manager dialog box again. The new scenarios appear on the list in the Scenarios box.

9. Select the desired Scenario Manager options. (*See* "Scenario Manager Options.")

10. Select a scenario and select Show to see how the scenario affects the model worksheet. All appropriate formulas will be recalculated to show the results of the changed cells.

11. Select Close to return to the worksheet.

12. Select Edit | Undo, or click on the Undo button on the Standard toolbar to restore the worksheet model to its original values.

Add Scenario Options

Comment
Record the user's name and date whenever a scenario is created or edited.

Prevent Changes
When worksheet protection is on, this option prevents unauthorized changes to the scenario.

Hide
When checked, the selected scenario name will not appear in the Scenario Manager dialog box.

Scenario Manager Options

Delete
Removes a highlighted scenario from the Scenarios list box.

Edit
Displays the Edit Scenario dialog box, which allows you to edit the scenario name, the changing cell references, comments, and scenario protection.

Merge
Displays the Merge Scenarios dialog box, from which you can merge scenarios from another worksheet in any open workbook.

Summary
Displays the Scenario Summary dialog box. You can create a separate worksheet with a scenario summary or pivot table report.

SELECTING

Selecting Cells and Objects

See SELECTING MENU ITEMS, COMMANDS, CELLS, AND OBJECTS in the section "The Mechanics of Using Excel 5."

Selecting Cells with Special Characteristics

To search a range of cells or the entire worksheet for cells that fit a particular description, and then select the cells:

1. Select the range of cells to be searched. If a range is not selected, the entire worksheet is searched.
2. Select Edit | Go To, or press F5. The Go To dialog box appears.
3. Select Special. The Go To Special dialog box appears.
4. Select the option that best describes the cells you want to locate.
5. Select OK or press ENTER to conduct the search. Each cell that fits the description is selected.

Selecting Two or More Worksheets in a Workbook

To group several worksheets together and apply formatting changes to all the selected worksheets at the same time:

- To select a group of adjacent worksheets, click on the tab of the first worksheet, press SHIFT and hold it down while you click on the tabs of the last worksheet. All worksheets between the first and the last are selected.

- To select a group of non-adjacent worksheets, press CTRL and hold it down while you click on the tab of each worksheet you want to be in the group.

- To ungroup selected worksheets, click on the tab of any worksheet not in the group.

Note   *You must have a mouse to select a group of worksheets. This feature is not available from the keyboard.*

SERIES

Filling a Range with a Series of Values

To fill a range of cells with a series of incremental values:

1. Enter the starting value or values into worksheet cells. Then select the range in which all the incremental values will appear. Be sure the starting values are in the first row or column of the selected range.

2. Select Edit | Fill | Series. The Series dialog box is displayed.

3. Select Rows or Columns to define where the incremental values will be entered.

4. Select the type of numerical series: Linear adds the step value to each cell; Growth multiplies the step value by each successive cell; Date creates a series of

dates; AutoFill fills the range based on the data included in the selected range.

5. If you select Date Unit, then select D_ay, _Weekday, _Month, or _Year to define the date progression.

6. Enter the _Step Value (defines the incremental change) and the St_op Value (defines where the series will stop).

7. Select OK or press ENTER to generate the series.

SOLVER

Solver adjusts the values in several cells in order to find the optimum value for a specific cell. Constraints can be applied to any of the adjusted values.

Solving a Formula with Multiple Variables

To solve a formula with multiple values:

1. Select the cell that contains the value to be maximized, minimized, or changed to a specific value. This cell should contain a formula.

2. Select _Tools | Sol_ver. The Solver Parameters dialog box appears. The selected cell appears in the Se_t Target Cell box. If you wish, type in another cell containing a formula.

3. Select _Max or Mi_n to set a maximum or minimum value for the formula. Select _Value of and type the desired value in the box.

4. Select _By Changing Cells and enter the cell addresses that you want changed. Select _Guess to have Excel suggest the changing cells.

5. Select _Add and enter the constraints for the cells to be changed in the Add Constraint dialog box. Constraints must include a cell reference, followed by a constraint operator, followed by the constraint. Click on the drop-down button and select a constraint from the list.

Select Add to add the constraint to the Subject to the Constraints list box. Repeat this procedure for each cell reference and select OK when finished. You will be returned to the Solver Parameters dialog box.

6. Select Change or Delete to edit or delete a highlighted constraint from the list.

7. If you're not happy with the constraints, select Reset All to clear all parameters and options from the dialog box.

8. Select Solve to generate the solution. The Solver Results dialog box appears. You can restore the original values or keep the values generated by the solver. You can also save the solver scenario for future reference using the Scenario Manager. You can also view a built-in solver report by selecting the desired report from the Reports list.

9. Select OK or press ENTER to exit the Solver.

Note   *The Solver command will only appear on the Tools menu if the Solver add-in has been installed and activated. See ADD-INS for instructions on activating an add-in.*

SPELL-CHECKING A DOCUMENT

To check the spelling of text in selected cells, a single worksheet, a group of worksheets, charts, text boxes, cell notes, headers and footers, buttons, and the formula bar:

1. Select the cells that contain the text to be spell-checked. If you select a single cell, the entire worksheet will be checked. To check a group of worksheets, select each worksheet to be checked.

2. Select Tools | Spelling; or click on the Spelling button on the Standard toolbar; or press F7. If an incorrect word is found, the Spelling dialog box appears.

3. Select the correctly spelled word from the Suggestions list. If the correct spelling does not appear on the list, type the correction in the Change To text box.

4. Select Ignore to bypass the word, or Ignore All to bypass every occurrence of the word.

5. Select Change to change the misspelled word to the word in the Change To text box, or Change All to change every occurrence of the misspelled word.

6. Select Add to add the word to the custom dictionary. You can have more than one custom dictionary. To create a new custom dictionary, type the dictionary name in the Add Words To text box. To select a custom dictionary, display the Add Words To drop-down menu and select the dictionary name. CUSTOM.DIC is the default custom dictionary.

7. When you're not sure how to spell a word, type an approximation into the Change To text box and select Suggest for a list of suggested spellings.

8. Turn on Ignore UPPERCASE to bypass words containing only uppercase letters.

9. Turn off Always Suggest if you don't want a suggestion list to automatically appear.

10. When the speller is finished, select OK or press ENTER.

SUMMARY INFO

Display information that describes the contents of a workbook and who created it. This information is useful when searching for files with the File | Find File feature.

1. Select File | Summary Info to display the Summary Info dialog box.

2. Type new entries or edit existing entries in the text boxes. *See* Summary Info options below.

3. Select OK or press ENTER when finished.

Note   *The Summary Info dialog box will be displayed when you save a workbook for the first time if you select Tools | Options to display the Options dialog box. Then select the General tab and check the Prompt for Summary Info box.*

Summary Info Options

Title
Type a descriptive title that makes it easy to identify the workbook.

Subject
Type a brief description of the contents of the workbook.

Author
Excel automatically inserts the name entered in the User Name box on the General tab. To insert or change a name, select Tools | Options, click on the General tab, and then type the name in the User Name box.

Keywords
Type any key words that might distinguish the contents of this workbook from other workbooks.

Comments
Type any additional comments that might be informative, especially for another user of the workbook.

STATUS BAR

Hiding and Viewing the Status Bar

To remove the status bar from the application window, and then redisplay it when needed:

- To hide the status bar, select View | Status Bar. When the status bar is displayed, there is a check mark in front of the Status Bar menu command. The status bar disappears from the bottom of the screen.

  Removing the status bar is helpful when you want to view more of the active worksheet.

- To display the hidden status bar, select View | Status Bar.

TABLE **103**

TABLE

A table is used to perform a "what if" analysis. A table has three elements: a formula that references an input cell, an input cell whose values will vary, and a list of values that will be substituted in the input cell. Values are substituted in one or two variables of a formula, or formulas, in order to see how the substituted values affect the results of the formula.

Generating a Data Table

You can create a one-input or two-input data table.

Creating a One-input Data Table

To create a one-input data table:

1. Enter the substitute values in a row or a column.

   These values will be substituted in place of the value in the input cell.

   If substitute values are in a column, the first formula must be in the cell that is directly above and one cell to the right of the first substitute value in the column. Additional formulas are placed in the row to the right of the first formula cell. If the substitute values are in a row, the first formula must be in the cell that is one cell directly below and to the left of the first value in the row of substitute values. Additional formulas are entered in the column of cells below the first formula.

2. Select a rectangular range that includes the formulas and substitute values.

3. Select Data | Table. The Table dialog box appears.

4. Select Row Input Cell if the substitute values are in a row. Select Column Input Cell if they are in a column. Then enter the input cell reference(s).

5. Select OK or press ENTER to compile a table of results.

Creating a Two-input Data Table

To create a two-input data table:

1. Enter the substitute values for one variable directly below the formula that refers to the two input cells, and the substitute values for the second variable directly to the right of the formula.

2. Select a rectangular range that includes the formulas and substitute values.

3. Select <u>D</u>ata | <u>T</u>able. The Table dialog box appears.

4. Select <u>R</u>ow Input Cell if the substitute values are in a row. Select <u>C</u>olumn Input Cell if they are in a column. Then enter the input cell reference(s).

5. Select OK or press ENTER to compile a table of results.

TEXT BOX

A text box is useful when you want to draw attention to specific text on a worksheet. Text in a text box can be treated as an object. The box and text can be formatted to enhance its appearance.

Creating a Text Box

To create a text box:

1. Click the Text Box button located on the Standard toolbar.

2. Place the mouse pointer where the box will be located, and then click and drag the mouse to form the shape of the box. To draw a perfectly square box, press SHIFT while dragging the mouse to shape the box.

3. Type text into the box. The text will wrap to the next line when it reaches the edge of the box.

4. Click anywhere on the worksheet when finished typing the text.

Editing a Text Box

To edit a text box:

1. To edit text in a text box, click on the box to select it.

2. Click a second time in the box. The insertion point will appear.

3. You can now edit the text as you would any other chart text.

Moving and Reshaping a Text Box

To move and reshape a text box:

1. To move a text box, click on the box and drag the box to a new location.

2. To reshape a text box, click on the box to select it. A gray border with handles appears around the box.

3. Drag any of the handles to reshape the box.

4. Click anywhere outside the box to return to the worksheet.

TIME VALUES

See NUMBERS, DATES, AND TIME VALUES, "Modifying the Appearance of Numbers, Dates, and Time Values."

TIPWIZARD

Displays helpful tips concerning an action you are currently performing. The lightbulb on the TipWizard button, on the Standard toolbar, will light up when the TipWizard has a tip for you.

1. To display the most recent tip, click on the TipWizard button on the Standard toolbar. You only receive a particular tip once during a work session. You will not see this tip again until you perform the operation associated with that tip three times.

2. To reset the TipWizard so another user can take advantage of recently displayed tips, select Tools | Options, select the General tab, and check the Reset TipWizard box.

TOOLBARS

Excel comes with several built-in toolbars containing buttons that help speed up many tasks. In addition to the built-in toolbars, you can create your own personal toolbars. In this section you'll learn how to display and hide a toolbar, create and delete a personal toolbar, and customize an existing toolbar.

Displaying and Hiding a Toolbar

To display and hide a toolbar:

1. Select View I Toolbars to display the Toolbars dialog box. A list of toolbars appears in the Toolbars list box. A check mark in a toolbar box indicates that the toolbar is currently displayed.

2. Place a check mark in the box for one or more of the toolbars you want to display. Remove the check mark from any toolbar you want to hide.

3. Select OK or press ENTER. The toolbar appears on your screen.

Note   *A fast way to display or hide a toolbar is to click the right mouse button on a toolbar to display a shortcut menu that lists all the available toolbars. Toolbars with a checkmark next to the name are currently displayed. Click on the name of any toolbar you want to display or hide.*

Customizing a Toolbar

To add or remove buttons from any toolbar:

1. Display on your screen the toolbar to be customized.

2. Select View I Toolbars to display the Toolbars dialog box and select Customize, or click the right mouse button on the toolbar and select Customize from the shortcut menu.

3. Select a category from the Categories list box. The buttons in that category are displayed. Click on a button to see a description for its use.

4. Drag a button to the toolbar being customized. To remove a button from the toolbar, drag the button onto the screen.

5. When you're finished, select Close.

6. If you want to return to the original configuration of a built-in toolbar, select View | Toolbars, select the customized toolbar, and then select Reset. Select OK or press ENTER.

Creating a Personal Toolbar

To create a personal toolbar:

1. Select View | Toolbars to display the Toolbars dialog box.

2. Type the personalized toolbar name in the Toolbar Name box and select Customize. The Customize dialog box appears along with an empty toolbar window in the upper-left corner of the screen.

3. Customize the toolbar according to the instructions in the previous section, "Customizing a Toolbar."

4. Select OK or press ENTER when finished.

Deleting a Personal Toolbar

To delete a personal toolbar:

1. Select View | Toolbars to display the Toolbars dialog box.

2. Highlight the name of the personal toolbar in the Toolbars list box.

3. Select Delete.

4. Select OK to verify the deletion, or Cancel if you change your mind.

Note *You can delete only a personal toolbar. You cannot delete a built-in toolbar.*

Positioning a Toolbar

To place a toolbar horizontally at the top or bottom of the screen or as a palette that you can move anywhere on the screen:

- When a toolbar is initially displayed, it usually appears horizontally across the top of the screen. Sometimes, however, a toolbar will appear as a palette. To move a palette, click anywhere on the palette other than a button and drag the palette to the new location.

- To turn a horizontal toolbar into a palette, click anywhere on the toolbar other than a button and drag the toolbar away from the top or bottom edge of the screen.

- To place a palette horizontally along the top or bottom of the screen, click anywhere on the toolbar other than a button and drag the toolbar against the top or bottom of the screen.

UNDOING AN EXCEL OPERATION

Undo, or reverse, the most recent operation. You are limited to undoing the last option selected, the last typed cell entry, or the last Undo operation.

1. Perform an operation from a menu or dialog box, type some text into a cell, or undo an operation.

2. Select Edit | Undo; click on the Undo button on the Standard toolbar; or press CTRL-Z.

Note *For operations that cannot be reversed, the grayed menu item Can't Undo appears on the Edit menu. You'll see Redo (u) instead of Undo on the Edit menu after you enter or edit data in a cell, select Undo to reverse that entry or edit, and then decide to restore the original entry or edit.*

UNGROUPING OBJECTS

See GROUPING AND UNGROUPING OBJECTS.

UNHIDING A WORKSHEET

See HIDING AND UNHIDING A WORKSHEET.

UNHIDING COLUMNS

See COLUMNS.

UNPROTECTING WORKBOOKS AND WORKSHEETS

See PROTECTING WORKBOOKS AND WORKSHEETS, "Unprotecting a Workbook or a Worksheet."

VIEW MANAGER

Record and display different views of a worksheet. A view includes all display settings, selected data, print settings, row heights, and column widths, plus window characteristics such as panes, frozen titles, and the window size and position. A view can also be displayed or printed without being saved as a separate document.

Creating Different Views

To create a different view of the worksheet:

1. Select View | View Manager to display the View Manager dialog box.
2. Select Add. The Add View dialog box appears.

3. Type a name for the view in the Name box.

4. In the View Includes area, mark the appropriate check boxes for the settings to be included in the view.

5. Select OK or press ENTER. You have just taken a photograph of the worksheet.

Displaying or Deleting a View

To display or delete a view:

1. Select View | View Manager to display the View Manager dialog box.

2. To delete a view, choose the view from the Views list and select Delete.

3. To display a view, select the view from the Views list and select Show.

Note *The View Manager command will not appear on the View menu unless the View Manager add-in has been installed and activated. See ADD-INS for instructions on activating the View Manager.*

VIEWING MORE OF THE WORKSHEET

To display more rows of a worksheet in the application window:

1. Select View | Full Screen. The worksheet fills the entire screen, with the menu bar along the top edge. The Standard and Formatting toolbars, the formula bar, and the status bar disappear. The Full Screen button appears in a palette.

2. To redisplay more of the application window, select View | Full Screen, or click on the Full Screen button.

WINDOWING TECHNIQUES

Activating an Open Window

Display a list of all open workbook windows when more than nine workbooks are open at the same time. You can then switch to the window you want to work in.

1. Select Window | More Windows. The Activate dialog box appears with a list of all open workbooks.

2. Choose the workbook you want to work on and select OK or press ENTER to display the chosen workbook.

Arranging Icons

Arrange all the minimized workbook windows along the bottom of the screen. This menu item only appears when all open workbook windows have been minimized into icons.

1. Select Window | Arrange Icons. The minimized icons sort themselves into rows along the bottom of the screen.

Arranging Open Windows

To arrange all open worksheets in an organized manner:

1. Select Window | Arrange to display the Arrange Windows dialog box.

2. Select the desired arrangement (*see* "Window Arrangements").

3. Select OK or press ENTER.

Window Arrangements

Tiled
Fits each window into a tiled mosaic similar to a tiled floor.

Horizontal
Stacks one window on top of another horizontally across the screen.

Vertical
Arranges each window vertically from left to right across
the screen.

Cascade
Overlaps open windows diagonally across the screen
from left to right.

Windows of Active Workbook
When selected, only the windows of the active workbook
are arranged. When cleared, all unhidden windows are
arranged.

Creating a Second Window for the Same Workbook

Create additional windows for an open workbook. Each
new workbook window will have the same name as the
original workbook, but will have a number added to the
name showing the numerical order of each workbook
window.

1. Select the open workbook for which you want to create
   additional windows.

2. Select Window | New Window. The additional window
   is displayed.

3. Continue repeating Step 2 to create as many copies of
   the open workbook window as you need.

Freezing and Unfreezing Panes

Prevent a designated area of a worksheet from scrolling,
allowing you to scroll through the rest of the worksheet and
still view the frozen area. This frozen area is called a *pane.*

Freezing a Pane

1. Select a cell below and to the right of the area that will
   be frozen.

2. Select Window | Freeze Panes. A horizontal and vertical line split the worksheet along the top and left edge of the selected cell. All data above the horizontal line is frozen when scrolling vertically, and all data to the left of the vertical line is frozen when scrolling horizontally.

Unfreezing a Pane

1. Select the worksheet that has been split.
2. Select Window | Unfreeze Panes. The horizontal and vertical lines disappear, allowing the entire worksheet to be scrolled.

Hiding and Unhiding a Workbook Window

Hiding a workbook is useful when you need several workbooks open at the same time and only want to work with a couple of them. Hide those less important workbooks so that switching between the more important workbooks is easier and faster. Hiding a workbook is also a good way to prevent accidental changes from being made to a workbook. A hidden workbook remains open.

Hiding a Workbook Window

To hide a workbook window:

1. Select the workbook to be hidden.
2. Select Window | Hide. The workbook disappears from view.

Unhiding a Workbook Window

To unhide a workbook window:

1. Select Window | Unhide. The Unhide dialog box appears with a list of currently hidden workbooks.
2. Choose the workbook to be unhidden and select OK or press ENTER. The document window appears.

Note   *If all open workbook windows have been hidden, the* Window *menu item will disappear from the main menu bar. To unhide a workbook in this case, select* File | Unhide.

Splitting and Unsplitting Windows

The active window can be split into four separate panes so that different parts of a worksheet can be viewed at the same time. The split can later be removed.

Splitting a Window

1. Select the active cell where the worksheet will be split.
2. Select Window | Split. Shaded bars appear along the top and left edges of the selected cell, splitting the document into panes. Additional scroll bars appear, allowing you to scroll through the panes.
3. Click on the horizontal or vertical bars and drag them to a new position to change the size of a pane.

Removing a Split from a Window

1. Select the split worksheet.
2. Select Window | Remove Split or double-click on any of the shaded bars. The bars disappear from the worksheet.

ZOOMING IN ON A DOCUMENT

To magnify or zoom in on a portion of the active document:

1. Select View | Zoom to display the Zoom dialog box.
2. Select the desired magnification, or type in a custom magnification in the Custom box. Select Fit Selection to zoom in on selected cells (select the cells prior to selecting Window | Zoom).
3. Select OK or press ENTER.

Working with a Chart

This section describes the features and commands necessary to create effective Excel charts.

3-D CHART

Changing the Viewing Angle

To change the viewing angle when working with a 3-D chart:

1. Select Format | 3-D View, or click the right mouse button on the chart and select 3-D View. The 3-D View dialog box is displayed.

2. Select the Elevation, Rotation, and Perspective buttons, or type the number of degrees in the text boxes, to change the view of the chart.

3. Check the Right Angle Axes box to display the chart axes at right angles, nullifying the current perspective settings.

4. Check the Auto Scaling box to automatically scale the 3-D chart to approximately the same size as the 2-D version of the same chart. Auto Scaling is only available when the Right Angle Axes box is checked.

5. If Auto Scaling is turned off, you can affect the height of the Y axis by selecting Height and typing a percentage value in the box. The Y axis height is measured as a percentage of the length of the X axis.

6. Select Apply to change the view without exiting the dialog box. You'll see the chart adjust to the new perspective.

7. Select Default to return the chart to its original default settings.

8. When you're satisfied, select OK or press ENTER to apply the changes and exit the dialog box (select Close or press ESC to exit without applying changes).

Formatting Floors and Walls of 3-D Charts

To change the color and the borders of the walls and floor of a 3-D chart:

1. Select the floor or wall area.
2. Select Format | Selected Floor or Selected Walls; double-click on the floor or walls; click the right mouse button on the walls or floor and select Format Walls or Format Floor; or press CTRL-1. The Format Floor or Format Walls dialog box appears.
3. Select the desired options from the Patterns options. *See* FORMATTING OPTIONS, "Patterns Tab Options," for details.
4. Select OK or press ENTER when finished.

ALIGNING CHART TEXT

To align chart titles, axis titles and labels, series labels, and so on:

1. Select the chart text.
2. Select Format | Selected; double-click on the chart text; click the right mouse button and select Format; or press CTRL-1. The Format dialog box appears.
3. Select the Alignment tab. The Alignment options vary depending on the type of text you selected.
4. Select the alignment options (*see* "Horizontal Options" and "Vertical Options").
5. Select OK or press ENTER when finished.

Horizontal Options

Left, Center, Right
Select one of these to align the selected chart text left, center, or flush-right within the text border.

Justify
Chart text is wrapped and aligned between the left and right edge of the text border.

Vertical Options

Top, Center, Bottom
Select one of these options to align the chart text along the top or bottom or in the center of the text border.

Justify
Spreads the text vertically between the top and bottom of the text border.

Orientation Options

Select the box that shows an example of how you want your text to appear on the chart.

ARROWS

Arrows are useful for directing attention to specific areas of a chart. You can add, move, resize, format, and delete chart arrows.

Note *You must have a mouse to add an arrow to a chart.*

Adding an Arrow

To add an arrow to a chart:

1. Select View | Toolbars and select the Drawing toolbar, or click the right mouse button on any active toolbar and select Drawing. The Drawing toolbar is displayed.

2. Click on the Arrow button. The mouse pointer turns into a crosshair.

3. Position the crosshair where the base of the arrow appears, drag the crosshair in the direction the arrow points, and release the mouse button. An arrow appears with a handle at each end.

4. Press ESC to remove the handles.

Moving and Resizing an Arrow

To move and resize a chart arrow:

1. Click on the arrow, or press any arrow cursor key until handles appear on the arrow.

2. To change the size of an arrow, click on either of the two handles and drag the arrow to the proper length.

3. To move an arrow, click on the shaft of the arrow and drag the arrow to the new location.

Deleting an Arrow

To delete a chart arrow:

1. Click on the arrow, or press any arrow cursor key until the handles appear on the arrow.

2. Press DEL. The arrow disappears.

Formatting an Arrow

To change the color, type, and size of an arrow:

1. Click on the arrow to be modified. To select more than one arrow, hold the SHIFT key down and click on each arrow.

2. Select Format | Selected Object; double-click on the arrow; click the right mouse button on the arrow and select Format Object; or press CTRL-1. The Format Object dialog box appears.

3. Select the Patterns tab and select the desired options (see "Patterns Options" and "Arrowhead Options").

4. To protect an arrow from being edited or moved, select the Protection tab and place a check mark in the Locked box. Remember, protection is not in effect until you activate protection for the chart sheet.

5. Select OK or press ENTER when finished.

Patterns Options

For a description of the Line options, *see* FORMATTING OPTIONS, "Patterns Tab Options."

Arrowhead Options

Style
Select from five different arrowhead styles on the drop-down list.

Width
Select from three different arrowhead widths on the drop-down list.

Length
Select from three different arrowhead lengths on the drop-down list.

AUTOFORMATTING A CHART

Change from one type of chart to another by applying a built-in autoformat. In addition to built-in autoformats, you can design and create your own user-defined autoformats.

Creating and Deleting a User-Defined Format

To create and delete a user-defined format:

1. Select the embedded chart or chart sheet that contains the formatting you want to turn into a user-defined autoformat.

2. Select Format | AutoFormat to display the AutoFormat dialog box.

3. Select User-Defined in the Formats Used area.

4. Select Customize. The User-Defined AutoFormats dialog box appears.

5. Select Add to display the Add Custom AutoFormat dialog box.

6. Type a name for the autoformat in the Format Name box and a description in the Description box. A name

can have up to 31 characters and a description can have up to 32 characters.

7. Select OK or press ENTER to return to the User-Defined AutoFormat dialog box. The new chart appears in the Format Sample box.

8. If you no longer need a particular user-defined autoformat, highlight the name and select Delete to remove it from the list.

9. Select Close or press ENTER to return to the worksheet or chart sheet. You can now apply the new autoformat to other charts.

Selecting a Built-In Autoformat

To select a built-in autoformat for a chart:

1. Select the embedded chart or chart sheet that you want to change.

2. Select Format | AutoFormat to display the AutoFormat dialog box.

3. Select Built-in in the Formats Used area. The built-in autoformats appear in the Galleries list box.

4. Select the desired chart category from the Galleries list box. All the available formats for that category appear in the Formats boxes.

5. Click on the desired format, or press the number above the format you want.

6. Select OK or press ENTER. Your previous chart is formatted according to the new format.

Selecting a User-Defined AutoFormat

To select a user-defined autoformat:

1. Select the embedded chart or chart sheet that you want to change.

2. Select Format | AutoFormat to display the AutoFormat dialog box.

3. Select Uuser-Defined in the Formats Used area. The built-in autoformats appear in the Formats list box.

4. Select the desired autoformat from the Formats list box. An example of the format appears on the screen.

5. Select OK or press ENTER. The chart is formatted according to the user-defined autoformat.

AXES

Displaying And Hiding Axes

To display or hide the X or Y axis of a chart:

1. Select Insert | Axes, or click the right mouse button anywhere on the chart or on any axis and select Insert Axes. The Axes dialog box appears.

2. To display an axis, select the appropriate axis box.

3. To hide an axis, unselect the appropriate axis box.

4. Click on OK or press ENTER.

Deleting an Axis

To delete a chart axis:

1. Select the axis to be deleted.

2. Select Edit | Clear | All, or press DEL. The axis disappears along with the axis labels and title.

Formatting an Axis

To modify the appearance of chart axes:

1. Select the category (Y), value (Y), value (Z), or series (Z) axis scale to be modified. The type of axis depends on the type of chart.

2. Select Format | Selected Axis; double-click on the axis; click the right mouse button on the axis and select Format Axes; or press CTRL-1. The Format Axis dialog box appears.

3. Select the appropriate dialog box tab, and then select the desired options (see the following sections).

4. Select OK or press ENTER when the modifications are completed.

Patterns Tab Options

Axis Area Options
See FORMATTING OPTIONS, "Patterns Tab Options," for a description of the Axis area options.

Tick Mark Type—Major and Minor
Select how you want the major and minor tick marks to appear along the chart axes, or turn them off.

Tick-Mark Labels
Select whether you want the tick-mark labels to appear at the low or high end of the axis or next to the axis, or if you want to turn them off.

The following options are found on the Scale dialog-box tab. A different Scale tab appears depending on which type of axis you select. Some of the options listed below will not be available depending on the type of chart currently in use.

Category (X) Axis Scale Options

Value (Y) Axis Crosses At Category Number
Determines where the value axis crosses the category axis.

Number of Categories between Tick Labels
Determines how many categories will appear between each tick-mark label along the scale line.

Number of Categories between Tick Marks
Determines how many categories will appear between each tick mark along the scale line.

Value (Y) Axis Crosses between Categories
Causes the value axis to cross the category axis between categories.

Categories in Reverse Order
Displays categories from right-to-left instead of
left-to-right.

Value (Y) Axis Crosses at Maximum Category
Causes the value axis to cross the category axis at the
maximum category.

Value (Y) Axis Scale Options

Minimum, Maximum, Major Unit, and Minor Unit
When the Auto boxes are checked, the highest and
lowest values along the value (Y) axis scale are
automatically determined based upon the chart values,
and the major and minor unit tick marks are automatically
placed along the appropriate axis. To specify axis values
and tick-mark distances, select the box to the right of the
item and type in the value.

Category (X) Axis Crosses At
When the Auto box is checked, the category axis crosses
the value axis at zero. Select the box to the right of the
item and type in a different value.

Logarithmic Scale
Displays a logarithmic scale along the value axis.

Values in Reverse Order
Displays values along the value axis from the top to the
bottom in ascending order.

Category (X) Axis Crosses at Maximum Value
Causes the category axis to cross the value axis at its
highest value.

Value (Z) Axis Scale Options

For 3-D charts with three axes, refer to "Value (Y) Axis
Scale Options" in the previous section for a description of
each option except the following:

Floor (XY Plane) Crosses At
Determines where the floor of the XY plane crosses the value (Z) axis.

Floor (XY Plane) Crosses At Minimum Value
Causes the XY plane to cross the value (Z) axis at the lowest value.

Series (Y) Axis Scale Options

These options are used to control the amount of space between tick marks, tick-mark labels, and gridlines along the series (Y) axis on 3-D charts.

Number of Series between Tick-Mark Labels
Determines how many series will appear between each tick-mark label along the scale line.

Number of Series between Tick Marks
Determines how many series will appear between each tick mark along the scale line.

Series in Reverse Order
Displays series from right-to-left instead of left-to-right.

Font Options

See FORMATTING OPTIONS, "Font Tab Options."

Number Options

See FORMATTING OPTIONS, "Number Tab Options."

Alignment Options

See FORMATTING OPTIONS, "Alignment Tab Options."

CHARTWIZARD

See CREATING A CHART.

CHART MENU BAR

The chart menu bar contains many commands that pertain specifically to charts and are not found on the main menu bar. To display the chart menu bar, double-click on a chart that is embedded in a worksheet, or select a chart sheet. The Data menu item is dropped from the menu bar and the remaining pull-down menus are altered for working with charts.

CHART TYPES

Change an existing chart type into another chart type. When you change a chart type, you change the way the data series is displayed. You can change the entire chart, or, if the chart contains more than one chart type, change only one of the chart types.

Changing the Entire Chart

To change a chart into an entirely different chart:

1. Select the chart that you want to change to another chart type.

2. Select Format | Chart Type, or click the right mouse button and select Chart Type to display the Chart Type dialog box.

3. If there are multiple chart types on the selected chart, select Entire Chart to change all the chart types to the new chart type.

4. Select one of the pictorial representations for the type of chart you want.

5. Select Options if you want to customize the chart settings, or to get a quick preview of what the new chart will look like. *See* FORMATTING CHART TYPE GROUPS for details about the available options.

6. Select OK or press ENTER when finished.

Changing a Chart Type on a Chart with Multiple Chart Types

1. Select the chart containing more than one chart type.
2. Select Format | Chart Type, or click the right mouse button and select Chart Type to display the Chart Type dialog box.
3. Select Group and choose the chart type group you want to change from the list.
4. Select one of the pictorial representations for the type of chart you want.
5. Select Options if you want to customize the chart settings or to get a quick preview of what the new chart will look like. *See* FORMATTING CHART TYPE GROUPS for details about the available options.
6. Select OK or press ENTER when finished.

Changing a Data Series into Another Chart Type

To change a selected data series into another chart type:

1. Select the data series on the chart to be changed.
2. Select Format | Chart Type, or click the right mouse button on the data series and select Chart Type, to display the Chart Type dialog box.
3. Selected Series should be selected. You can still elect to change a chart type group or the entire chart if you wish.
4. Select the pictorial representation for the type of chart type you want.
5. Select OK or press ENTER. The data series is transformed into a new chart type.

Note *A quick way to change a chart type, whether it be the entire chart or a chart type group, is to select the chart or chart group and click on the arrow for the Chart Type* *drop-down list. A pictorial representation of each chart type is displayed. Then select the desired chart type and watch the data series immediately change. If you click directly on the Chart Type button on the Chart toolbar, the selected chart or data series is immediately changed to the type of chart displayed on the Chart Type button.*

COLOR

Modifying Chart Colors

To change the color of chart objects:

1. Select the chart element for which you want to change the color.

2. Select Format | Selected [*object*]; click the right mouse button on the object and select Format [*object*]; or press CTRL-1. The format dialog box for the selected chart object appears.

3. Make the desired edits from either a color drop-down list or a palette, whichever is appropriate for the options available in the dialog box.

4. Select OK when finished.

Note   *If you don't like the new color, immediately select Edit | Undo or click on the Undo button to restore the previous color.*

CREATING A CHART

Charts are created with the ChartWizard. The ChartWizard creates a chart by leading you step-by-step through a series of five dialog boxes. You can create a chart embedded in a worksheet, or you can create a separate chart sheet.

Creating an Embedded Chart

To insert a chart into an existing worksheet:

1. Choose one of the two ways to initiate the creation of an embedded chart. The first way is to select the range of worksheet data to be transformed into a chart, and then select Insert | Chart | On This Sheet. The second way is to first select Insert | Chart | On This Sheet, and then select the range, as explained in Step 2. The mouse pointer changes into a crosshair with a small chart symbol.

2. Place the crosshair on the worksheet where you want the chart to appear and click the mouse button. The first ChartWizard dialog box appears with the selected range appearing in the Range box. If you used the second method in Step 1, you have to type in the range to be charted, or select the range directly on the worksheet.

3. You can select Finish at any time when you are satisfied with the construction of the chart. To make additional choices about the chart, select Next to display the next dialog box. Select Back to return to the previous dialog box.

4. Select the type of chart you want and then select Next. The third dialog box appears.

5. Select the format for the chart style and then select Next. The fourth dialog box appears.

6. Select the Sample Chart options (see the following section) for how you want the data to be displayed. The pictorial representation of the chart reflects each option you select. When satisfied, select Next. The fifth, and final, dialog box appears.

7. Select the Sample Chart options (see the following section) for how you want the data to be displayed.

8. Select Finish when you are satisfied with all your choices. The chart appears in your worksheet.

Note *If you want to let Excel do the work, a fast method of creating an embedded chart is to click on the arrow next to the Chart Type button on the Chart toolbar and select one of the 14 types of charts. Then select the worksheet data to be charted, click directly on the Chart Type button, place the mouse crosshairs on the worksheet, and click. A chart is immediately created and inserted into the worksheet. You'll then have to edit the chart to suit your needs. See CHART TYPES for more details on changing chart types.*

Sample Chart Options— Step 4 of 5 Dialog Box

The options vary depending on the type of chart you have selected.

Rows
Data series will be plotted from rows.

Columns
Data series will be plotted from columns.

Use First Columns
Specify the columns from the selected worksheet data that will be used to supply (X) axis labels, pie and doughnut slice labels, or radar axis labels.

Use First Rows
Specify the rows from the selected worksheet data that will be used to supply titles for the legend text, pie chart title, doughnut series titles, or surface (Y) axis labels.

Sample Chart Options— Step 5 of 5 Dialog Box

Add a Legend?
Indicate whether you want to add a legend.

Chart Title
Type a title for the chart.

Axis Titles
Type a title for each axis. A grayed-out axis is not available on the chart.

Creating a Chart Sheet

Create a chart on a separate sheet in a workbook. The chart sheet is linked to its source data and is updated when you change the source data.

1. Follow steps 1 through 5 in the section "Creating an Embedded Chart," except that in Step 1 you'll select Insert | Chart | As New Sheet instead of selecting Insert | Chart | On This Sheet.

2. When you've completed work with the ChartWizard, select Finish. A new chart sheet is inserted in the workbook.

Creating a Combination Chart

Display chart data as more than one chart type on the same chart. For example, the chart could have several data series presented as columns and another set of data series displayed as data points connected by a line. This creates an overlay effect; thus this type of chart is sometimes referred to as an overlay chart.

1. Follow steps 1 through 5 in the section "Creating an Embedded Chart," except that in Step 4 you'll select the chart type titled Combination.

2. When you've completed work with the ChartWizard, select Finish. A new chart sheet is inserted in the worksheet.

3. You may want to make some changes to the way ChartWizard formatted the chart. Refer to CHART TYPES for information about changing a chart type.

DATA SERIES AND POINTS

This section shows you how to incorporate additional worksheet data as data series or points in an existing embedded chart or chart sheet.

Adding Data Series or Points to a Chart Sheet

To add additional data series or points to a chart:

1. Select the worksheet data to be added to the chart.
2. Select Edit | Copy; click on the Copy button on the Standard toolbar; or click the right mouse button and select Copy.
3. Switch to the chart sheet.
4. Select Edit | Paste, or click on the Paste button on the Standard toolbar. The data is automatically incorporated into the chart.

Note *If Excel is ever uncertain about where to place the data, the Paste Special dialog box appears. You can then specify whether the data is a series or points. Dialog box options vary depending on whether you are adding cells as a new data series or as points to an existing data series in the chart.*

Adding Data Series or Points to an Embedded Chart

To add additional data series or points to a chart:

1. Double-click on the chart to activate it.
2. Select Insert | New Data. The New Data dialog box appears.

3. Type in the new range, or select the range directly on the worksheet.

4. Select OK or press ENTER. The new data is immediately incorporated into the chart.

Note *The fastest way to add new data series or points to an embedded chart is to select the worksheet data, click on the border of the selected range, and drag the range onto the chart. The chart is automatically updated with the new data.*

Deleting a Data Series

To delete a data series from a chart:

1. Select the series.

2. Select Edit | Clear | Series. The series is removed from the chart.

Changing the Order of a Data Series

To place a data series in another location on the axis:

1. Select the chart you want to edit.

2. Select Format to display the pull-down menu. The chart group appears at the bottom of the menu. The name of the group depends on the type of chart you are working with.

3. Select the [*chart type*] group to display the Format [*chart type*] Group dialog box.

4. Select the Series Order tab. *See* FORMATTING CHART TYPE GROUPS, "Series Order Tab Options," for details on the Series Order options.

5. Select OK or press ENTER when finished.

Formatting a Data Series

To format a data series:

1. Select the series.

2. Select Format | Selected Series; double-click on the series; click the right mouse button on the series and

select Format Series; or press CTRL-1. The Format Data Series dialog box appears.

3. Select the appropriate dialog box tab, and then select the desired options. *See* FORMATTING OPTIONS for a description of the tab options.

4. Select OK or press ENTER when finished.

DELETING A CHART OBJECT

See OBJECTS, "Removing a Chart Object."

EDITING CHART TEXT AND VALUES

Editing Chart Text

To edit chart and axis titles, data labels, and text boxes:

1. Select the text to be edited. Handles appear around the body of the text.

2. Immediately type new text that will replace the existing text. You can also place the mouse pointer over the text; when the pointer turns into an I-beam, click the mouse and an insertion point appears in the text. You can now make discrete edits to the text.

Note *If you edit text on the chart that is linked to source data in a worksheet, the links will be lost. It is best if you edit linked text at the source so that the chart text will be updated automatically.*

Editing Chart Values

To change the values on an existing chart:

1. Select the worksheet that is linked to the chart.

2. Edit the values on the worksheet that are the source for the chart values. The chart values are automatically updated.

Note *On some chart types, you can change a chart value by clicking once on the data series that represents the value to be changed and then clicking one more time on the data series to activate the data marker. Drag the data marker up or down in the direction you want the value to change. The changing value will be displayed at the far left of the formula bar as you drag the data marker. If you drag a data marker that represents a value with a formula, the Goal Seek dialog box will appear. Type the cell reference for the cell containing the value that needs to be changed in order for the chart data point to arrive at the desired result.*

ERROR BARS

Error bars are used to indicate the degree of uncertainty for plotted chart data.

Creating Error Bars

To create error bars:

1. Select the data series to which the error bars will be applied.
2. Select Insert | Error Bars, or click the right mouse button on the series and select Insert Error Bars to display the Error Bars dialog box.
3. Select the desired options (see the following section).
4. Select OK or press ENTER when finished.

Note *Error bars cannot be added to pie, doughnut, radar, or 3-D charts.*

X and Y Error Bars Tab Options

Display

Select the style of error bars you want to appear on the chart. Select none if you do not want to display error bars.

Fixed Value

Type a fixed value that will be used as the error amount for all data points.

Percentage

Click on the up and down arrows or type a percentage value that will be calculated from each data point to be used as the error amount.

Standard Deviations

Click on the up and down arrows, or type the number of standard deviations from the mean for plotted values to be used as the error amount.

Standard Error

Select this option to use the standard error of the plotted values as the error amount for each data point.

Custom

Type a range of values that are equal in number to the data points in the series. You can also select the range directly off the worksheet by dragging the mouse. Enter values in both the plus and minus boxes, or select Both in the Display area.

Formatting and Editing Error Bars

To format and edit error bars:

1. Select the error bar you want to format.
2. Select Format | Selected Error Bars; double-click on the error bar; click the right mouse button on the error bar and select Format Error Bars; or press CTRL-1. The Format Error Bars dialog box appears.

3. To format the error bars, select a new marker from the Patterns tab. *See* FORMATTING OPTIONS, "Patterns Tab Options," for more details. To edit the error bars, select the Y Error Bars tab and make the appropriate changes. *See* "Creating Error Bars" for more details about these options.

4. Select OK or press ENTER when finished.

FONTS

Changing a Font Style, Size, and Color for a Chart

An interesting font can enhance the appearance of chart and axis titles, category and data labels, and legend text. When changing to a new font, you can select the entire chart area or specific objects such as axes, legends, titles, and so on.

1. Select the chart area or object that contains the text to be enhanced.

2. Select Format | Selected; double-click on the chart area or object; click the right mouse button on the object and select the Format option; or press CTRL-1. The Format dialog box for the selected area or object appears.

3. Select the Font tab and select the desired options. *See* FORMATTING OPTIONS, "Font Tab Options," for a description of the font options available on the Font tab.

4. Select OK or press ENTER to apply the changes and close the dialog box.

FORMATTING CHART TYPE GROUPS

The Group command is located at the bottom of the Format menu. The name of the Group command changes depending upon the type of chart that you have selected, such as a Line Group or a Column Group.

To format a Group chart:

1. Select the chart.
2. Select Format to display the pull-down menu and select [*chart type*] Group from the bottom of the menu, or click the right mouse button on the chart and select Format [*chart type*] Group.
3. The Format [*chart type*] Group dialog box appears.
4. Select the desired options from the Group tabs (see the following sections).
5. Select OK when finished.

Subtype Tab Options

Subtype
Select one of the chart subtypes. A subtype is just another way of looking at the same type of chart.

Series Order Tab Options

These options allow you to place a data series at another location on the axis.

Series Order
Highlight the series that you want to reposition.

Move Up or Move Down
Moves the selected series into the desired location.

Options Tab Options

The options on the Options Tab vary according to the type of chart you are working with.

Overlap
Type or click on the arrow buttons to set the percentage of overlap for the bars and columns in 2-D bar and column chart groups.

Gap Width
Type or click on the arrow buttons to set the amount of space between bars and columns on 2-D and 3-D bar and column charts.

Gap Depth
Type in or click on the arrow buttons to set the distance between the data markers in all 3-D charts. (This does not work with surface charts.)

Chart Depth
Type in or click on the arrow buttons to set the depth of a 3-D chart.

Series Lines
Check this box to connect the data markers for each chart series with lines. This option only works with stacked bar and column chart groups.

Vary Colors By Point/Slice/Category
Check this box to assign a different color or marker to each data marker. This option only applies to chart type groups with a single data series.

Drop Lines
Check this box to draw a line between each marker and the X axis in an area or line chart group.

Up-Down Bars
Check this box to create high-low ranges for opening and closing prices on a high-low line chart.

High-Low Lines
Check this box to draw high-low lines between the highest and lowest values in each category on a high-low chart. This option only works for 2-D line chart groups.

Radar Axis Labels
Check this box to display category axis labels for radar chart groups.

Angle Of First Slice

Type in a number or click on the arrow buttons to establish the angle in degrees at which the first pie or doughnut slice starts.

Doughnut Hole Size

Type in or click on the arrow buttons to specify the size of the hole in a doughnut chart group.

Axis Tab Options

Select either a primary or secondary axis for one or all of the data series on one chart type. *See* FORMATTING OPTIONS, "Axis Tab Options," for details on these options.

FORMATTING OPTIONS

This section provides a brief description of most of the formatting options available in Excel. Because Excel formatting options are generally available on tabs within dialog boxes, and many of these tabs are common to many of Excel's formatting features, this section is organized by tabs.

Alignment Tab Options

Click on the text alignment box that best shows how you want your text to look.

Horizontal Text Alignment

Select Left, Center, or Right to align text left, center, or flush-right within the selected text borders. Justify aligns text between the left and right edge of the text borders.

Vertical Text Alignment

Top, Center, and Bottom align data with the top, center, or bottom edges of the text borders. Justify spreads the text vertically between the top and bottom of the text borders.

Orientation
Controls the orientation of selected chart text. If there is too much text to format into a single line, Microsoft Excel wraps the text into lines. If a chart axis is selected, this option controls the orientation of the tick-mark labels.

Automatic
Select this option to restore the default orientation to axes labels.

Automatic Size
Select this option to restore an altered orientation to the default orientation for text boxes.

Axis Tab Options
Select either a primary or secondary axis for one or all of the data series on one chart type.

Primary Axis
The selected data series or chart type group is plotted along the primary axis.

Secondary Axis
The selected data series or chart type group is plotted along the secondary axis.

Chart Type and Options Buttons
Select these to switch between the Chart Type and Format Group dialog boxes. The Chart Type dialog box allows you to change the chart type.

Data Label Tab Options
None
Data labels will not be displayed. Existing data labels will be cleared from the chart.

Show Value
The value of the data point is displayed.

Show Percent
The percentage of the whole is displayed for a pie or doughnut chart.

Show Label
The category assigned to the data point is displayed. Also, series names are displayed on area charts.

Show Label and Percent
Percentages of the whole and the category or series names are displayed for pie and doughnut charts.

Show Legend Key Next To Label
The legend is located near the data label.

Font Tab Options

Font
Select the desired font from the list.

Font Style
Select a font style from the list.

Size
Select a size from the list, or, if the size you want does not appear on the list, type it in. A sample appears in the Preview box.

Underline
Select single, double, or no underlining from the drop-down list.

Color
Select a text color from the drop-down palette, or select Automatic to choose the color set in the Windows Control Panel.

Background
Select Automatic to apply the default background, Transparent to leave the area behind the chart text

transparent, and Opaque to remove a pattern but leave the foreground color behind the text.

Normal Font
Sets the font style, size, and effects to the normal style, which is the style used on all sheets until another style is applied.

Effects
Check Strikethrough, Superscript, or Subscript to apply these special effects to the text.

Name and Values Tab Options

Name
The name of the selected data series appears in the Name box. You can type a name in the box, designate an absolute cell reference, or enter a name previously defined for a single cell. The name appears in the legend.

Y Values
Type the cell references for the values for the data series selected in the Series box, or select the range directly off the worksheet. You can also enter a named range.

Number Tab Options

Category
Select the category that corresponds to the type of number you're working with.

Format Codes
Select the appropriate format code for the selected category. This code appears in the Code box.

Code
Create a custom format code by editing an existing code or by typing in the format directly.

Linked to Source
Check to link the chart values to source data on another worksheet.

Patterns Tab Options

Use to enhance the appearance of lines, borders, axes, markers, and fill areas.

The Pattern tab options are divided into areas depending on the Excel feature. These areas include Border, Line, Axis, Marker, Area, and Fill:

- Border options apply style, color, and weight to the lines that form borders around many chart items.

- Line options apply custom styles, colors, and weights to most lines found on a chart.

- Axis options apply custom styles, colors, and weights to axes lines and their tick marks. (*See* AXES, "Formatting an Axis," for a description of tick-mark labels and types.)

- Marker options apply custom styles, foregrounds, and backgrounds to error bars. They apply data markers in radar, line, and XY charts.

- Area/Fill options apply patterns, pattern colors, and fill colors to certain areas within charts and objects. These items include the chart and plot areas, many data markers, walls and floors on 3-D charts, and so on.

Border/Line/Axis Options

Automatic

Applies the default Style, Color, and Weight to lines, arrowheads, and axes. Also formats and places the default border around certain chart items.

None

Selected borders and lines hidden, with the exception of gridlines.

Custom Style

Select from eight different styles on the drop-down list.

Custom Color

Select from 56 different colors and patterns on the drop-down palette.

Custom Weight
Select from four different thicknesses on the drop-down list.

Shadow
Places a shadow around the border of the object.

Smoothed Line
Creates smoother, less angular, lines on an XY or line chart.

Round Corners
Corners are rounded on borders of text boxes.

Area and Fill Options

Automatic
The default fill pattern is applied to the chart object.

None
The area is displayed without a fill pattern.

Color
Select a color to fill the area surrounding the item or object.

Pattern
Select a pattern for the fill.

Invert if Negative
Enhance negative values by reversing the foreground and background fill patterns.

Marker Options

Automatic
Applies the default pattern to the marker.

None
Hides the data markers.

Custom Style
Select from the drop-down list one of several symbols to represent a data marker.

Custom Foreground
Select from the drop-down palette a foreground color for the fill.

Custom Background
Select from the drop-down palette a background color for the fill.

X Values Tab Options

X Values
Type the cell references that contain the category tick-mark labels, or select them directly from the worksheet. You cannot do this with pie, doughnut, and XY charts.

GRIDLINES

Adding and Removing Gridlines

Add or remove gridlines from a chart. A chart can have major and minor gridlines.

1. Select Insert | Gridlines, or click the right mouse button on the chart and select Insert Gridlines. The Gridlines dialog box appears. You can click on the Horizontal Gridlines button on the Chart toolbar, but this will only display or hide the major gridlines for the value axis.

2. Select the appropriate check boxes for the gridlines you want to appear on the chart (*see* the following section, "Gridline Options").

3. Select OK or press ENTER.

Note *You can change the gridline spacing. Double-click on the gridlines to display the Format Gridlines dialog box, select the Scale tab, and then make the changes you want.*

Gridline Options

Major Gridlines
Displays or hides major gridlines from the specified axis.

Minor Gridlines
Displays or hides minor gridlines from the specified axis.

2-D Walls and Gridlines
Causes gridlines to appear two-dimensionally on 3-D bar and column charts.

INSERTING A PICTURE IN A CHART

See INSERTING PICTURES in the section "Working with Workbooks and Worksheets."

LABELS

Adding Data Labels

Add labels to data series and data points. The data labels are picked up from the worksheet; you do not type them in.

1. Select the data point or the data series.
2. Select Insert | Data Labels. The Data Labels dialog box appears.
3. Select the data label options that determine how the data will look on the chart (see the following section, "Data Labels Options").
4. Select OK or press ENTER when finished.

Note   *Once a label is added to the chart, it can be edited. However, the link with the worksheet will be broken.*

Data Labels Options

None
Data labels will not appear on the chart. Existing labels will no longer appear with the data series or points.

Show Value
The numerical value of a data series or point is displayed.

Show Percent
The labels will display a value equal to a percentage of the whole for pie and doughnut charts.

Show Label
The name of the series category, as it appears on the axis, is displayed at each data point. The data series name will be displayed for area charts.

Show Label and Percent
The labels will display both a value equal to a percentage of the whole pie and the series or category name for pie and doughnut charts.

Automatic Text
If you edit a data label and break its link to the worksheet, you can restore the link with this option. Check this box and select OK, and the labels will once again reflect the source data on the worksheet.

Show Legend Key Next To Label
The legend key will appear next to the data label.

Deleting Data Labels

See OBJECTS, "Removing a Chart Object."

Formatting Data Labels

To format data labels:

1. Select the label to be formatted.
2. Select Format | Selected Data Labels; double-click on the data label; click the right mouse button and select Format Data Labels; or press CTRL-1. The Format Data Labels dialog box appears.
3. Select the desired formatting options. *See* FORMATTING OPTIONS for a description of these options.
4. Select OK or press ENTER to return to the chart.

LEGENDS

The instructions in this section guide you through adding, deleting, moving, and resizing a chart legend.

Adding a Legend

To add a legend to a chart:

1. Select the embedded chart or chart sheet.
2. Select Insert | Legend, or click on the Legend button on the Chart toolbar. The legend is automatically created and placed on the chart.

Deleting a Legend

To delete a chart legend:

1. Select the chart legend and press DEL, or click on the Legend button on the Chart toolbar. The legend disappears from the chart.

Changing the Legend Location and Appearance

To change the location of a legend and modify the appearance of the legend:

1. Select the chart legend. Handles appear around it.

2. Click anywhere on the legend and drag the legend to the desired location. You also can select Format | Selected Legend; double-click on the legend; click the right mouse button on the legend and select Format Legend; or press CTRL-1. The Format Legend dialog box appears.

3. Select the Placement tab and select where you want the legend to appear on the chart.

4. Select OK or press ENTER.

Moving and Resizing a Legend

See OBJECTS, "Moving and Resizing a Chart Object."

Formatting a Legend

To format a legend:

1. Select the legend.

2. Select Format | Selected Legend; double-click on the legend; click the right mouse button and select Format Legend; or press CTRL-1. The Format Legend dialog box appears.

3. Select the desired options. *See* FORMATTING OPTIONS, "Patterns Tab Options" and "Font Tab Options," for details.

4. Select OK or press ENTER when finished.

LINKING CHART DATA

To link a chart or axis title or a text box to a cell on a worksheet:

1. Select the title or text box.

2. Type an equal sign (=) into the formula bar. Then type the worksheet cell reference, or select it directly on the chart with the mouse.

3. Press ENTER. The worksheet cell is now linked to the chart text. When you edit the text in the worksheet cell, the linked text on the chart is automatically updated.

MOVING A CHART OBJECT

See OBJECTS, "Moving and Resizing a Chart Object."

OBJECTS

Moving and Resizing a Chart Object

To move a chart object from one location to another:

1. Select the object to be moved. Handles appear around it.
2. To move the object, click anywhere on the object and drag it to the desired location.
3. To resize the object, click on any handle and drag the object into the desired shape.

Removing a Chart Object

To delete an object or its formatting from a chart:

1. Select the chart object.
2. Select Edit | Clear to display the submenu.
3. Select one of the three options (see the following section, "Clear Options"). A grayed-out option on the submenu is not available.

Clear Options

All

Deletes the selected chart object and its formatting. If you select the chart area, all the chart items are deleted, leaving a blank area where the chart was located.

<u>Series</u>/<u>T</u>rendline/Error Bars
Depending on which of these chart objects is selected,
you can delete the selected data series or data points, the
trendline, or the error bars.

<u>F</u>ormats
Removes the formatting from any selected chart item; the
data is not affected.

Selecting a Chart Object

To select a chart object:

1. Click on the desired object. Objects include axes, labels,
titles, legends, and floors and walls of 3-D charts.
Handles appear on the selected object.

PROTECTING AND UNPROTECTING CHARTS

The chart protection feature allows you to assign a
password to a worksheet or workbook that contains an
embedded chart or a chart sheet. A protected chart
cannot be viewed or edited.

Protecting an Embedded Chart or Chart Sheet

See PROTECTING WORKBOOKS AND WORKSHEETS,
"Protecting an Open Workbook" and "Protecting a
Worksheet," in the section "Working with Workbooks and
Worksheets."

Unprotecting a Chart

See PROTECTING WORKBOOKS AND WORKSHEETS,
"Unprotecting a Workbook or a Worksheet," in the section
"Working with Workbooks and Worksheets."

RENAMING A CHART SHEET

See NAMING A WORKSHEET IN A WORKBOOK in the section "Working with Workbooks and Worksheets."

SCALES

See AXES, "Formatting an Axis."

SELECTING CHART AREAS AND OBJECTS

Selecting a Plot or Chart Area

Select an area of a chart for the purpose of editing or formatting that area. The *plot area* forms the background for the plotted data series. The *chart area* forms the backdrop for the entire chart, including all titles, labels, and legends.

- To select the plot area, click anywhere on the area directly behind and bordering the plotted data series. Handles appear around the area.

- To select the chart area, click anywhere on the outer edges of the background area for the entire chart. Handles appear around the outer edges.

Note   *To unselect any selected area or object, press* ESC.

Selecting a Chart Object

See OBJECTS, "Selecting a Chart Object."

Note   *To unselect any selected area or object, press* ESC.

SERIES

See DATA SERIES AND POINTS.

SIZING A CHART OBJECT

See OBJECTS, "Moving and Resizing a Chart Object."

SPELL-CHECKING A CHART

See SPELL-CHECKING A DOCUMENT in the section "Working with Workbooks and Worksheets."

TITLES

Creating Chart Titles

Place titles on certain areas of a chart. These areas include the chart title, values along the Y axis, categories along the X axis, or a data series.

1. Select the chart to which you want to add titles.
2. Select Insert | Titles, or click the right mouse button on the chart and select Insert Titles. The Titles dialog box is displayed.
3. Select one or more of the axes that you will assign a title.
4. Select OK or press ENTER. Temporary titles, called *placeholder text*, are entered on the chart.
5. Select the placeholder text and type the actual title.
6. Press ESC when finished to deselect the title.

Editing Chart Titles

See EDITING CHART TEXT AND VALUES.

TRENDLINES

Add a line showing the trend or direction of flow of a group of chart data. Trends are useful for developing moving averages. The trendline must be associated with data series in column, bar, area, line, and scatter chart groups.

Note   *Trendlines cannot be created on pie, doughnut, 3-D, or radar charts.*

Creating a Trendline

To create a trendline on a chart:

1. Select the data series for which you want to show a trend.
2. Select Insert | Trendline, or click the right mouse button on the series and select Insert Trendline, to display the Trendline dialog box.
3. Select the desired options (see the following sections).
4. Select OK or press ENTER when finished. The trendline appears on the chart.

Type Tab Options

Trend/Regression Type

Select the pictorial representation for the type of trendline appropriate for your chart. Type the polynomial order, a number between 2 and 6, in the Order box. When calculating a moving average, type the number of periods used for the calculation.

Options Tab Options

Automatic
The trendline is automatically named after the type of trend selected on the Type tab, followed by the name of the series.

Custom
Type a custom name for the trendline.

Forward and Backward
Click on the up or down arrows or type the number of periods—or the number of units, when working with an XY chart—that will be projected into the future or away from the Y axis (Forward), or into the past or toward the Y axis (Backward).

Set Intercept
Check this box and type the point where the trendline and the Y axis meet.

Display Equation On Chart and Display R-Squared On Chart
Check these boxes if you want to display the regression equation, the R-squared value, or both in the trendline label.

Editing and Formatting a Trendline

To edit and format a trendline:

1. Select the trendline on the chart.
2. Select Format | Selected Trendline; double-click on the trendline; click the right mouse button on the trendline and select Format Trendline; or press CTRL-1. The Format Trendline dialog box appears.
3. To format the trendline, select the desired Patterns options. *See* FORMATTING OPTIONS, "Patterns Tab Options," for details. To edit the trendline, select the appropriate options from the Type and Options tab.

4. Select OK or press ENTER to return to the chart.

UNPROTECTING A CHART

See PROTECTING WORKBOOKS AND WORKSHEETS, "Unprotecting a Workbook or a Worksheet," in the section "Working with Workbooks and Worksheets."

Working with a List

This section describes the features available to you when working with lists of related data. Lists are useful for organizing large amounts of data so that you can extract needed information in a quick and efficient manner. A list can also serve as a database.

ADDING A RECORD

See RECORDS, "Adding a Record."

AUTOFILTER

See FILTERING A LIST, "Filtering with AutoFilter."

CONSTRUCTING A LIST

Construct a list that contains *records*, which are entered into worksheet rows, and *fields*, which are entered into worksheet columns. Each record can contain an item from each field.

1. Type the label for each field into adjacent cells in a row (field items will be typed in the column below each label). Field entries should be related, and the field label should indicate the type of information entered in the field. For example, if you name a field ADDRESS, each cell under that name should contain an address.

2. The data for each record is then typed in the rows below the field labels. The field data along a row should relate to a single subject, such as a single customer or a single company.

3. Select the list range and give it a name. This makes it easier to locate the list and perform list-management operations. The range should include all the cells containing the list entries and the field labels. (See NAMES, "Defining a Name" or "Using the Name Box," in the "Working with Workbooks and Worksheets" section.)

Hints and Reminders

- Limit a worksheet to a single list to make list management easier.

- Leave a blank row and column surrounding the list.

- Filtered data will obscure worksheet data on the left or right of the list.

- Data entered into list columns should have the same cell formatting. However, the column labels should have a different format, alignment, font, data type, pattern, and border than the data entered in the fields.

- Do not type extra spaces in front of the data typed into a cell, because the spaces will interfere with sorting and searching for the data.

CRITERIA RANGE

See FILTERING A LIST for a discussion on creating a criteria range and working with search criteria.

DATA FORMS

See RECORDS for information on using a data form.

DELETING A RECORD

See RECORDS, "Deleting a Record."

FILTERING A LIST

Search for and display specified types of data from a list.
Only the filtered data is displayed on the worksheet,
while the rest of the data in the list is hidden from view.
You can filter a list using the AutoFilter command or by
applying advanced search criteria for a more sophisti-
cated filter. After data has been filtered, you can edit,
sort, print, and create a chart from the filtered
information.

Filtering with AutoFilter

To filter data from a list with AutoFilter:

1. Select any cell in the list.

2. Select Data | Filter | AutoFilter to turn the AutoFilter
   feature on. A set of drop-down arrows appears next to
   each column label for the fields of data.

3. Click on an arrow to drop down a list of items unique to
   the fields under that column.

4. Select an item from the list. All records containing the
   selected item are immediately displayed. The unfiltered
   information is hidden.

5. If you want to filter the data according to customized
   search criteria, select Custom from the drop-down list
   to display the Custom AutoFilter dialog box. Then
   select the custom criteria (see "Custom AutoFilter
   Criteria") for that particular column, and then select OK
   or press ENTER to filter the list.

6. To turn AutoFilter off, select Data | Filter | AutoFilter
   again. The checkmark next to the AutoFilter command
   means AutoFilter is turned on.

Custom AutoFilter Criteria

These criteria allow you to search for records containing
two field items, or to search for records containing data
that falls between two values.

- Select the search items from the drop-down lists, or type the items directly into the boxes.

- Select a logical operator from the drop-down list to the left of the search item boxes. (See the note following "Advanced Filtering" for a description of logical operators.)

- Select And to filter records containing both items.

- Select Or to filter records containing either the first search item or the second search item.

Advanced Filtering

With advanced filtering, you type the search criteria directly into cells on the worksheet. This is called the *criteria range*. The criteria range consists of two or more rows with labels in the first row and search criteria typed into the cells below the labels. The labels must match exactly the column labels in the list. Place the criteria range just above or below the list so that the list of records remains in view.

1. Type the criteria labels into the first row of the criteria range.

2. Type the search criteria for each label in the cell directly below the label. You can use logical operators (see the note following this list) and wildcards (?, *, ~).

3. Place the active cell anywhere in the list and select Data | Filter | Advanced Filter. The Advanced Filter dialog box appears. The entire list is automatically selected to be searched.

4. To narrow the search range, select List Range and type in the new range, or drag the mouse over the range.

5. Select Criteria Range and type in the cell references for the criteria range, or drag the mouse over the range.

6. If you want to copy the results of the filter to another location in the same worksheet or into another worksheet, select Copy to Another Location and type in the new location in the Copy to box.

7. Check the Unique Records Only box to exclude any rows that contain duplicate data.

8. Select OK or press ENTER. The filtered data appears in place or in the selected location.

9. To restore the list to the way it looked before the filter operation, select Data | Filter | Show All.

Note *You can use relational operators to restrict the search to specified parameters. The operator must be typed in front of the search criteria. The operators include < (less than), > (greater than), = (equal to), <= (less than or equal to), >= (greater than or equal to), and <> (not equal to).*

FINDING A RECORD

See RECORDS, "Finding a Record."

RECORDS

You will want to make changes to a list when records need to be added, deleted, and edited. You can perform these operations directly on the list, but you might find it easier to use the data form. The data form is a dialog box that displays all the fields of a selected record.

Note *A list must have column labels in order for you to use the data form.*

Adding a Record

To add a record to a list:

1. Place the active cell on the list.

2. Select Data | Form. The data form dialog box appears. The dialog box takes on the title of the worksheet.

3. Select New to clear the field boxes.

4. Type the data for the new record into the field boxes.

5. Select Close to insert the new record at the bottom of the list. You will have to sort the list to place the records in the correct order.

Deleting a Record

To delete a record from a list:

1. Place the active cell on the list.

2. Select Data | Form to display the data form dialog box.

3. Locate the record to be deleted.

4. Select Delete. You are alerted that the record will be deleted permanently from the list.

5. Select OK to delete the record.

Editing a Record

To edit a record in a list:

1. Place the active cell in the list.

2. Select Data | Form to display the data form dialog box.

3. Locate the record to be edited. You can click on the scroll arrows or press the up and down arrows to display the next record. Press PGUP or PGDN to move ten records at a time. Press CTRL+PGUP to move to the top of the list and CTRL+PGDN to move to the end of the list.

4. Make the edits in the field boxes. If a field cannot be edited, the data will not appear in a field box.

5. Select Restore to cancel any edits made to a field. You must do this before selecting another record or selecting Close.

Finding a Record

To locate a record in a list:

1. Place the active cell on the list to be searched.

2. Select Data | Form. The data form dialog box appears.

3. Select Criteria. The field boxes are cleared and the scroll bar is whited out, which indicates that it can no longer be used for scrolling.

4. Type the search criteria into the desired field boxes. You can use logical operators (<, =, >, <=, >=, <>).

5. Select Find Next or Find Prev to locate the next occurrence of a record that meets the search criteria.

6. To once again use Find Next and Find Prev to move through the entire list, select Criteria and select Clear to erase the search criteria from the field boxes. Then click on Form to display the list records. If you suddenly change your mind, select Restore to recover the search criteria before selecting Form.

PIVOT TABLES

A pivot table is a table used for summarizing and analyzing data from an existing list. A pivot table is updated when the source data in the list is changed. A pivot table can be created from source data located in an Excel list, in another pivot table in the same Excel workbook, in multiple Excel consolidation ranges, or in an external database created in another application external to Excel.

Adding a Field to a Pivot Table

To add a row, column, or page field to an existing pivot table:

1. Place the active cell on the pivot table.

2. Select Data | PivotTable, or click the right mouse button on the pivot table and select PivotTable. The PivotTable Wizard—Step 3 of 4 dialog box appears.

3. Drag the new fields onto the layout diagram.

4. Select Finish. The pivot table is updated to reflect the added fields.

Changing the Pivot Table Summary and Calculation Method

To change the function used to summarize a data field, and to select a new calculation type that is used for calculating the values in a data field:

1. Select a cell in the column or row of the field for which you want to change the summary function and/or calculation type.

2. Select Data | PivotTable Field, or click the right mouse button on the pivot table and select PivotTable Field. The PivotTable Field dialog box appears with the summary function and field name in the Name box.

3. If needed, change the name of the selected data field by typing a new name in the Name box. The new name will replace the old name on the pivot table.

4. To change the summary function, select the desired function in the Summarize by box.

5. Select Delete to delete the summary information for the selected field from the pivot table.

6. Select the Number button to format the values in the data field.

7. To change the way values are calculated, select the Options button. A new set of options appears at the bottom of the PivotTable Field dialog box.

8. Select the desired options (see "PivotTable Field Options").

9. Select OK or press ENTER.

PivotTable Field Options

These options let you create a customized calculation procedure for the data field. A custom calculation compares the data field information with a field and an item in the pivot table.

Show Data As
Select a calculation type from this list. The selected function will be used to compare a set of pivot table data with another set of related data.

Base Field
Select a base field from the list of fields that appear in the pivot table. The data in this field will be the base data with which related data will be compared.

Base Item
Select an item from the base field. This item will be the base item used in the calculation. Select (previous) or (next) to have each calculation use the value preceding or following the current item in the base field.

Clearing a Pivot Table

To erase a pivot table from the worksheet without affecting the source data:

1. Select the entire pivot table range.
2. Select Edit | Clear | All.

Note *You cannot move or clear a portion of a pivot table. You can, however, copy data from a pivot table for use elsewhere.*

Creating a Pivot Table

Create a table that summarizes selected categories of data according to a specified method of calculation. Row entries are summarized on the right side of the pivot table; column entries are summarized at the bottom. You can change the orientation of the table by moving the row and column headings to different locations around the source data, thereby creating a new table to reflect the new orientation. You can create a pivot table from any worksheet data that has labeled columns.

1. Determine which fields you want to appear in the table, and which items you want from those fields. Field names are the column labels.

2. Select Data | PivotTable to display the PivotTable Wizard—Step 1 of 4 dialog box. You can select Finish at any time and a pivot table will be created based on the information you've given the PivotTable Wizard up to that point.

3. Select the source of the data to be used in the pivot table and select Next to move to the PivotTable Wizard—Step 2 of 4 dialog box.

4. Select Range and type in the range of source data, or select it directly from the worksheet by dragging the mouse over the data. When the data has been identified, select Next to move to the PivotTable Wizard—Step 3 of 4 dialog box.

Note If you are creating a pivot table from external data, multiple worksheet ranges, or another pivot table, you will see slightly different dialog boxes. Follow the instructions in the dialog boxes to locate the source data.

5. Drag the field buttons into the pivot table layout. Where you place the field will determine how the source data is compared, tabulated, and summarized. You can change the location of a field directly on the worksheet if you don't like the results. When you're satisfied with the field placement, select Next to display the PivotTable Wizard—Step 4 of 4 dialog box.

6. Select PivotTable Starting Cell and type in a cell address, or select it directly off the worksheet with the mouse.

7. Type a name for the pivot table in the PivotTable Name box.

8. Place a check in the box for each of the PivotTable Options you want.

9. Select Finish to generate the pivot table on your worksheet.

Removing a Field from a Pivot Table

Remove a row, column, or page field from an existing pivot table. The fields are those cells that have a gray-shaded background. These cells, with the exception of the Data field, can be removed directly from the pivot table.

1. Select the field to be removed from the pivot table.
2. Drag the field out of the pivot table range. The field turns into a gray bar with an **X** over it.
3. Release the mouse button and the field is removed from the pivot table.

Reorganizing a Pivot Table

Rearrange the data in a pivot table. You cannot edit the data in the pivot table, but the fields can be moved into new positions so that you get a different view of the data.

1. Select the field you want to arrange differently.
2. Drag the field to either a row, column, or page orientation. The pivot table automatically reorganizes itself to display the data in the new orientation.

Updating a Pivot Table

To refresh a pivot table when the data in the source list has been changed:

1. After the data in the list is changed, place the active cell in the pivot table.
2. Select Data | Refresh Data, or click the right mouse button on the pivot table and select Refresh Data. You are alerted that the pivot table was changed during the Refresh Data operation.
3. Select OK.

Updating a Pivot Table After Adding Rows or Columns

To refresh a pivot table when new rows or columns have been added:

1. After the new rows or columns have been added, place the active cell in the pivot table.

2. Select Data | PivotTable, or click the right mouse button on the pivot table and select PivotTable. The PivotTable Wizard—Step 3 of 4 dialog box appears.

3. Select Back to display the PivotTable Wizard—Step 2 of 4 dialog box.

4. Select Range and type the new range, including the additional rows and columns, or select the range directly on the worksheet by dragging the mouse.

5. Select Finish to update the pivot table with the new data.

PROTECTING A LIST

See PROTECTING WORKBOOKS AND WORKSHEETS in the section "Working with Workbooks and Worksheets" for details on protecting worksheet data.

SORTING A LIST

To sort list records alphabetically, numerically, or chronologically:

1. Select the range to be sorted. You can select the entire list or only part of the list. If you've given the list a name, drop down the name list by clicking on the arrow on the formula bar and selecting the name for the list.

2. Select Data | Sort to display the Sort dialog box.

3. Select the sort options (see "Sort Options").

4. Select Ascending or Descending, depending on the order in which you want the data to be sorted.

5. Select OK or press ENTER to sort the selected records.

Note *Excel uses the following sort order for ascending sorts: numbers, text and text that includes numbers, logical values, error values, and blank cells. This order is reversed for a descending sort, except for blank cells. Blank cells are always the last to be sorted.*

Sort Options

Sort By
Select the column you want to sort by from the drop-down list and select either the ascending or descending sort order.

Then By and Then By
Select these boxes to specify the order in which to sort rows when there are duplicate items in the column specified in Sort By. Also, select either the ascending or descending sort order.

My List Has
Select Header Row if the list has column labels. Select No Header Row to include in the sort the first row in a list without column labels.

Advanced Sort Options

Select the Options button to display the Sort Options dialog box. These advanced options allow you to customize the sort procedure.

First Key Sort Order
Drop down the menu list and select a built-in or custom sort order for the column you specified in the Sort By box in the Sort dialog box. You can add a customized sort order to this list by selecting Tools I Options, selecting the Custom Lists tab, and creating a new list.

Case Sensitive
Sort duplicate items according to case: all uppercase first, leading uppercase second, and all lowercase last.

Sort Top To Bottom
Sort data or rows by a single column.

Sort Left To Right
Sort data or columns by a single row.

Working with Macros

A macro consists of a series of recorded keystrokes and commands that execute a particular task. When the macro is played back, Excel automatically performs that task. Macros are handy time-savers when you need to perform routine operations on a regular basis.

ASSIGNING MACROS

You can run a macro quickly by assigning it to a graphic object, a button, or a toolbar tool, or by assigning it to the Tools pull-down menu. Running macros in this manner can make your job go faster and easier.

Assigning a Macro to a Button

Assigning a macro to a worksheet button is a two-phase operation; first you create the button and then you assign the macro. To run the macro, simply click on its assigned button. The button is available whenever the worksheet is open.

To assign a macro to a button:

1. Display the Drawing toolbar.
2. Click on the Create Button tool.
3. Place the mouse pointer where you want the button to appear, drag the button into the desired shape and size, and release the button. The Assign Macro dialog box appears.
4. Select the macro from the list or type a macro name in the Macro/Name Reference box and then select OK or press ENTER. Select Record if you want to record a new macro (see RECORDING A MACRO).
5. To type a new label on the button, hold down CTRL and click on the button to select it. Then click on the button

again to place an insertion point in the text. Make your edits and then click anywhere on the worksheet.

Note   *To select the button so it can be moved, resized, or deleted, press* CTRL *while clicking on the button. You can also use the* F*ormat* I *Obj*e*ct command to customize the button.*

Assigning a Macro to an Object

To assign a macro to an object:

1. Create the object to which the macro will be assigned and then click on the object to select it.

2. Select T*ools* I Assi*gn* Macro to display the Assign Macro dialog box.

3. Select the macro from the list or type a macro name in the M*acro/Name* Reference box and then select OK or press ENTER. Select R*ecord* if you want to record a new macro (see RECORDING A MACRO).

4. When you click on the object, the macro will run.

Assigning a Macro to a Toolbar Button

Macros assigned to a toolbar can be used in all worksheets in any workbook. You can assign a macro to a built-in toolbar button or to a custom button. If you use a built-in button, the assigned macro will override the task normally assigned to that button.

Built-In Button

To assign a macro to a built-in button on a toolbar:

1. Display the toolbar with the button to which you want to assign a macro.

2. Select V*iew* I T*oolbars* to display the Toolbars dialog box.

3. Click the desired button on the actual toolbar. See TOOLBARS, "Customizing a Toolbar," in the section "Working with Workbooks and Worksheets" for information on placing a new button on a toolbar.

4. Select Tools | Assign Macro to display the Assign Macro dialog box.

5. Select the macro from the list or type a macro name in the Macro/Name Reference box and select OK or press ENTER. Select Record if you want to record a new macro (see RECORDING A MACRO).

6. Select OK or press ENTER to return to the Toolbars dialog box.

7. Select OK or press ENTER.

Note *To return the toolbar button to its original task, select View | Toolbars, select the toolbar, and then select Reset.*

Custom Button

To assign a macro to a custom button on a toolbar:

1. Display the toolbar to which a macro will be assigned.

2. Select View | Toolbars to display the Toolbars dialog box.

3. Select Customize and add a button from the Custom category to the desired toolbar. (For additional information, see TOOLBARS, "Customizing a Toolbar," in the section "Working with Workbooks and Worksheets.") The Assign Macro dialog box appears.

4. Select the macro from the list or type a macro name in the Macro/Name Reference box.

5. Select OK or press ENTER to return to the Customize dialog box.

6. Select Close. Now, when you click on that button, the assigned macro will run.

Note *To return the custom toolbar button to its original task, select View | Toolbars, select the toolbar from the list, and then select Reset. To remove the custom button from the toolbar, see TOOLBARS, "Customizing a Toolbar," in the section "Working with Workbooks and Worksheets."*

Assigning a Macro to the Tools Menu

To assign a macro to the Tools menu:

1. Select Window | Unhide to display the workbook in which the macro is stored.

2. Select Tools | Macro, or click on the Run Macro button on the Visual Basic toolbar, to display the Macro dialog box.

3. Select the macro from the list or type a macro name in the Macro/Name Reference box.

4. Select Options. The Options dialog box appears.

5. Check the Menu Item on Tools Menu box and type in the name of the macro as it will appear on the Tools menu.

6. Select OK or press ENTER. The Macro dialog box appears.

7. Select Close. The macro name will now appear at the bottom of the Tools pull-down menu.

Changing a Macro Assigned to a Worksheet Button or Object

There may be times when you will want to change a button or object that already has a macro assigned to it. You can assign a different macro or delete the existing macro.

To assign a different macro to a button or object, or to delete an existing macro:

1. Select the worksheet button or object (remember to hold down CTRL) to which a macro has been assigned.

2. Select Tools | Assign Macro to display the Assign Macro dialog box.

3. To change a macro, select a different macro from the list or type a macro name in the Macro/Name Reference box. To delete a macro, delete the name from the box, which will remove the current macro from the object. Select Record if you want to record a new macro (see RECORDING A MACRO).

4. Select OK or press ENTER.

DEBUGGING A MACRO

When a macro does not run correctly, an error message appears on the screen and the macro module is displayed with the malfunctioning macro instruction. You can run the malfunctioning macro one step at a time to evaluate it for misspellings, typos, incorrect commands, and so on.

1. Run the desired macro. An error box appears, telling you what Excel thinks the problem is. The macro module sheet is displayed behind the error box with the erroneous code highlighted.

2. Correct the error directly on the module sheet.

3. Select Run | Step Into (F8) or Step Over (SHIFT-F8), or click on the Step Into or Step Over buttons on the Visual Basic toolbar. The debugger will place a box around the first line of code where you can begin making changes, if needed.

4. Continue to select Run | Step Into or Step Over. Step Into goes to the next line of code so it can be analyzed. Step Over works the same as Step Into, except that it will execute the next line of code if it is a call to a procedure, and then it will move on to the next line of code.

5. When you finish stepping through the macro and correcting any other errors, the macro fully executes.

Note   You can run any macro through the debugging process by selecting Tools | Macro or clicking on the Run Macro button on the Visual Basic toolbar, selecting the macro to be debugged, and then selecting Step. The Debug window opens and you can step through the macro.

DELETING A MACRO

To delete a macro:

1. Select Tools | Macro, or click on the Run Macro button on the Visual Basic toolbar, to display the Macro dialog box.

2. Select the macro to be deleted from the list, or type a macro name in the Macro/Name Reference box.

3. Select Delete. The macro is deleted from the list and the Visual Basic module sheet where it was stored.

EDITING A MACRO

Before you can edit a macro, the workbook where the macro is stored must be open. Macros are written on a worksheet called a Visual Basic module. Edits are made directly on the macro module sheet.

1. Select Tools | Macro, or click on the Run Macro button on the Visual Basic toolbar, to display the Macro dialog box.

2. Select a macro from the list, or type a macro name in the Macro/Name Reference box and select OK or press ENTER.

3. Select Edit. The module sheet appears on the screen.

4. Make the needed edits to the macro.

5. Select File | Save to save the changes.

ERROR MESSAGE WHEN RUNNING A MACRO

If an error occurs when you are running a macro, an error box is displayed on the screen. Press the Debug button and refer to DEBUGGING A MACRO for details on what to do.

OPTIONS

Changing Options for Existing Macros

There are several options you can change after creating a macro without having to recreate the macro from scratch.

To change options for an existing macro:

1. Select Tools | Macro, or click on the Run Macro button on the Visual Basic toolbar, to display the Macro dialog box.

2. Select the macro from the list or type a macro name in the Macro/Name Reference box.

3. Select Options. The Options dialog box appears.

4. Make the desired changes. See RECORDING A MACRO for details about each option.

5. Select OK or press ENTER when finished.

6. Select Close to return to the worksheet.

RECORDING A MACRO

A macro is created when you turn the macro recorder on and type keystrokes and select commands. These actions are recorded for playback at a future time.

To record a macro:

1. Plan the keystrokes and commands for the procedure that will comprise the macro.

2. Select Tools | Record Macro | Record New Macro, or click on the Record Macro tool on the Visual Basic toolbar. The Record New Macro dialog box appears.

3. Select Macro Name and enter a name for the macro. A name must start with a letter and can be up to 255

characters long (including underscores, but no spaces or punctuation marks).

4. Type a description of the macro in the Description box.

5. Select the Options button and select the desired options from the list below.

6. Select OK or press ENTER to begin recording the macro.

7. Perform the keystrokes and select the commands that comprise your planned macro. All of your actions will be recorded in the macro.

8. When finished recording the macro, select Tools | Record Macro | Stop Recording, or click on the Stop Recording tool on the Visual Basic toolbar.

Record New Macro Options

Menu Item on Tools Menu

Check this box to place the macro on the Tools pull-down menu. Type a macro name in the text box. This name appears on the pull-down menu.

Shortcut Key

Check this box and type a letter (it must be a letter) in the CTRL box. Press CTRL-[letter] to run the macro.

Store in

Select Personal Macro Workbook to store the macro in a workbook titled PERSONAL. Select This Workbook to store the macro in the active workbook. Select New Workbook to store the macro in a new workbook.

Language

Select Visual Basic to create the macro in the Visual Basic language native to Excel 5.0. Select MS Excel 4.0 Macro to create the file in the Excel 4.0 language.

Note Macros recorded on the Personal Macro Workbook are available at all times because the file is automatically opened, but hidden, when you start Excel. If you record a macro with the This Workbook or New Workbook options, be sure to save those workbooks with the File | Save command. Otherwise the macros won't be available in the future.

RECORDING USING ABSOLUTE AND RELATIVE REFERENCES

You can record a macro using either relative or absolute references. Recording a macro using relative references causes a macro to operate on cells a set distance from the active cell, no matter where the active cell is located. A macro recorded using absolute cell references causes the macro to operate on the same cells every time. The default setting is relative references.

To record a macro using either relative or absolute cell references:

1. Select Tools | Record Macro, or click on the Record Macro button on the Visual Basic toolbar, to display the submenu. Check to see if the Use Relative References command has a check mark next to it. If so, relative references are in use. If there is no check mark, absolute references are in use.

2. Select Use Relative References to replace or remove the check mark, toggling between absolute and relative references.

REPEATING A MACRO

This is a quick way to repeat a macro that isn't assigned to a button or object.

1. Run the macro and then reposition the active cell where you want to repeat the macro.

2. Select Edit | Repeat Macro; click on the Repeat button on the Standard toolbar; or press F4. The macro immediately executes again.

RUNNING A MACRO

To run a macro simply means to play back the same keystrokes and command selections you made when you recorded the macro.

To run a macro:

1. Select the worksheet location where you want the macro to execute.

2. Select Tools | Macro, or click on the Run Macro button on the Visual Basic toolbar. The Macro dialog box appears.

3. Choose a macro from the list box or type the name of a macro in the Macro Name/Reference box. If you type a macro name, be sure to type the macro sheet name, an exclamation mark, and then the name of the macro, with no spaces between these entries.

4. Select OK or press ENTER to run the macro. If there is an error in the macro, an error box appears on the screen. See DEBUGGING A MACRO for more details.

SHORTCUT KEY

Setting or Changing the Macro Shortcut Key

A shortcut key lets you run a macro by pressing two keys from the keyboard. You cannot assign a shortcut key to a macro when you initially create it, but you can assign a shortcut key to the macro later on. Also, you may want to change a shortcut key that has already been assigned.

To set or change a shortcut key:

1. Select <u>T</u>ools | <u>M</u>acro, or click on the Run Macro button on the Visual Basic toolbar, to display the Macro dialog box.

2. Select the desired macro from the list or type in the macro name.

3. Select <u>O</u>ptions. The Macro Options dialog box appears.

4. Check the Shortcut <u>K</u>ey box and type the letter to be used with the CTRL key in the Ct<u>r</u>l+ box.

5. Select OK or press ENTER. The Macro dialog box appears.

6. Select Close to return to the worksheet.

STOPPING A MACRO WHILE IT'S RUNNING

To stop a macro that is currently running, click on the Stop Macro button on the Visual Basic toolbar. To resume running the macro, click on the Resume Macro button.

UNHIDING AND HIDING A MACRO WORKBOOK

See WINDOWING TECHNIQUES, "Hiding and Unhiding a Workbook Window," in the section "Working with Workbooks and Worksheets."

Toolbar Reference

This section provides a quick-reference guide to the buttons found on the Excel toolbars. The quick-reference guide is divided into ten sections, with each section devoted to a single toolbar. There are ten categories of toolbars: Standard, Formatting, Chart, Drawing, Forms, Auditing, Visual Basic, Workgroup, Query and Pivot, and Microsoft.

STANDARD TOOLBAR

Button	Name	Description
	New Workbook	Opens a new workbook
	Open File	Opens an existing workbook
	Save File	Saves a workbook
	Print	Prints a document
	Print Preview	Previews the document prior to printing
	Spelling	Checks for spelling errors

Button	Name	Description
	Cut	Removes selected data or object and places it into the Clipboard
	Copy	Copies selected data or object and places it into the Clipboard
	Paste	Places Clipboard data or object into the document
	Format Painter	Copies only the formatting from a selection
	Undo	Reverses the most recent command or action
	Repeat	Repeats the last action
	AutoSum	Enters the SUM function with a proposed range
	Function Wizard	Displays the Function Wizard dialog box and pastes the selected function into the active cell or formula bar
	Sort Ascending	Sorts selected data in ascending order
	Sort Descending	Sorts selected data in descending order

Button	Name	Description
	Chart Wizard	Starts the ChartWizard
	Text Box	Uses crosshairs to draw a text box
	Drawing	Displays the Drawing toolbar
	Zoom Control Box	Changes the display scale of the document
	TipWizard	Displays helpful tips
	Help	Displays help for a specific topic. After clicking this tool, place the mouse pointer and question mark on a command or worksheet area and click again for help with that topic.

FORMATTING TOOLBAR

Button	Name	Description
	Font Box	Selects a font from the available fonts list
	Font Size Box	Selects a font size from the available font size list
	Bold	Turns bold formatting on or off for selected cells

Button	Name	Description
I	Italic	Turns italic formatting on or off for selected cells
U	Underline	Turns underline formatting on or off for selected cells
	Align Left	Aligns data to the left
	Align Center	Aligns data in the center
	Align Right	Aligns data to the right
	Center Across Columns	Centers data across selected columns
$	Currency Style	Applies the currency style to selected cells
%	Percent Style	Applies the percent style to selected cells
,	Comma Style	Applies the comma style to selected cells
+.0 .00	Increase Decimal	Adds a decimal place for each click of the tool

Button	Name	Description
	Decrease Decimal	Decreases a decimal place for each click of the tool
	Borders	Selects a border style from a palette of borders
	Color	Changes the color of an object or cell
	Font Color	Changes the color of selected text

CHART TOOLBAR

Button	Name	Description
	Chart Type	Selects one of 14 chart types
	Default Chart	Changes a selected chart to the default type as specified on the Chart tab
	Chart Wizard	Starts the ChartWizard
	Horizontal Gridlines	Adds or deletes gridlines along the value axis
	Legend	Adds or deletes a legend

DRAWING TOOLBAR

Button	Name	Description
	Line	Draws a straight line
	Rectangle	Draws a rectangle or square
	Ellipse	Draws an ellipse or a circle
	Arc	Draws an arc
	Freeform	Draws an object that includes straight lines and freehand lines
	Text Box	Draws a text box in which text can be typed
	Arrow	Draws an arrow on a worksheet or a chart
	Freehand	Draws a continuous freehand line
	Filled Rectangle	Draws a rectangle or square filled with a color or pattern

Button	Name	Description
	Filled Ellipse	Draws an oval or circle filled with a color or pattern
	Filled Arc	Draws an arc filled with a color or pattern
	Filled Freeform	Draws an object that includes straight lines and freehand lines and is filled with a color or pattern
	Create Button	Draws a button on a worksheet
	Drawing Selection	Changes mouse pointer to an arrow for selecting objects
	Bring to Front	Moves an object in front of all other objects
	Send to Back	Moves an object to the rear of all other objects
	Group Objects	Combines selected objects into a single object
	Ungroup Objects	Separates objects in a group into discrete objects
	Reshape	Changes the shape of a polygon

Button	Name	Description
	Drop Shadow	Places a shadowed border around selected cells or objects
	Pattern	Changes the pattern color of a selection

AUDITING TOOLBAR

Button	Name	Description
	Trace Precedents	Draws arrows from value-supplying cells directly to their related formula in the active cell
	Remove Precedent Arrows	Deletes trace-precedent arrows
	Trace Dependents	Draws arrows from the active cell directly to those cells containing formulas that are affected by the values in the active cell
	Remove Dependent Arrows	Deletes dependent-tracer arrows
	Remove All Arrows	Deletes all tracer arrows
	Trace Error	Draws an arrow from a cell that might have caused an error value in the active cell

Button	Name	Description
	Attach Note	Attaches a note or audio comment to the active cell
	Show Info Window	Displays the Info window

WORKGROUP TOOLBAR

Button	Name	Description
	Find File	Displays the Find File dialog box
	Routing Slip	Adds routing information to the current notebook
	Send Mail	Attaches a workbook to electronic mail
	Update File	Updates a read-only file to the previously saved version
	Toggle File Status	Switches between read-write and read-only
	Scenarios	Displays, adds, and edits scenarios

FORMS TOOLBAR

Button	Name	Description
	Label	Creates a text label
	Edit Box	Creates an edit box
	Group Box	Creates a group box
	Create Button	Creates a button on a worksheet, chart, or dialog sheet
	Check Box	Creates a check box
	Option Button	Creates an option button
	List Box	Creates a list box
	Drop-Down	Creates a drop-down list box
	Combination List-Edit	Creates a combination list and edit box
	Combination: Drop-Down Edit	Creates a combination drop-down list and edit box

Button	Name	Description
	Scroll Bar	Creates a scroll bar
	Spinner	Creates a spinner control
	Control Properties	Changes the properties of the worksheet controls on the Control tab
	Edit Code	Creates or edits code for a selected object
	Toggle Grid	Displays and hides alignment gridlines
	Run Dialog	Runs the custom dialog box currently being edited on a dialog sheet

VISUAL BASIC TOOLBAR

Button	Name	Description
	Insert Module	Inserts a new macro module in the current workbook
	Menu Editor	Creates and edits an Excel menu

Button	Name	Description
	Object Browser	Browses through the objects, procedures, methods, and properties in the active worksheet
	Run Macro	Runs a macro
	Step Macro	Goes through each step of a macro while it runs
	Resume Macro	Continues running a paused macro
	Stop Macro	Stops a macro from running and stops the recording of a macro
	Record Macro	Records a macro
	Toggle Breakpoint	Sets or removes a breakpoint
	Instant Watch	Displays the value of the selected Visual Basic expression
	Step Into	Steps to the next line of Visual Basic code
	Step Over	Steps to the next line of Visual Basic code, but runs other call procedures

MICROSOFT TOOLBAR

Button	Name	Description
	Microsoft Word	Runs Microsoft Word
	Microsoft Powerpoint	Runs Microsoft Powerpoint
	Microsoft Access	Runs Microsoft Access
	Microsoft FoxPro	Runs Microsoft FoxPro
	Microsoft Project	Runs Microsoft Project
	Microsoft Schedule+	Runs Microsoft Schedule+
	Microsoft Mail	Runs Microsoft Mail

QUERY AND PIVOT TOOLBAR

Button	Name	Description
	PivotTable Button	Starts the PivotTable Wizard

Button	Name	Description
	PivotTable Field Button	Inserts a subtotal for either a selected row field or column field in a pivot table. Also, if you select a cell in the data area, you can define the summary functions used to calculate the values in the data field.
	Ungroup Button	Separates items in a combined group or removes selected rows or columns from a group
	Group Button	Creates a group from selected detail rows or columns. Also groups multiple items in a pivot table into a single item
	Hide Detail Button	Hides detail data in a pivot table. Also hides the detail rows or columns within a selected group
	Show Detail Button	Displays hidden detail data in a pivot table. Also shows the detail rows or columns within a selected group
	Show Pages Button	Copies each page of a page field to a new worksheet
	Refresh Data Button	Reruns the query on data imported with Microsoft Query and then inserts the results in the result set. (The active cell must be in the result set.) Also, when the active cell is in a pivot table, updates the pivot table data when the source data is changed

Excel Functions

Excel functions are listed alphabetically in the following table. Each listing includes the function name, required and optional arguments, and a brief description of what the function returns when it is implemented. Optional arguments appear in brackets ([]). If an argument is followed by an ellipsis (...), it means that you can include more arguments than are shown in the table.

Note *If you are entering a function in a formula and need a quick reference to the function's arguments, type an equal sign, the function name, and the opening parenthesis, and then press* CTRL-A.

Function	Returns
ABS(*x*)	Absolute value of *x*
ACCRINT(*issue,first_interest, settlement,coupon,*[*par*], *frequency,*[*basis*])	Accrued interest for security that pays interest periodically
ACCRINTM(*issue,maturity, coupon,*[*par*],[*basis*])	Accrued interest for security that pays interest upon maturation
ACOS(*x*)	Arccosine of *x*
ACOSH(*x*)	Inverse hyperbolic cosine of *x*
ADDRESS(*row_num,column_num,* [*abs_num,a*],[*sheet_text*])	The cell address as text
AND(*logical1,logical2,*...)	TRUE if arguments are TRUE
AREAS(*reference*)	Number of areas (single ranges) in *reference*
ASIN(*x*)	Arcsine of *x*
ASINH(*x*)	Inverse hyperbolic sine of *x*
ATAN(*x*)	Arctangent of *x*

Function	Returns
ATAN2(*x,y*)	Arctangent of *x* and *y* coordinates
ATANH(*x*)	Inverse hyperbolic tangent for *x*
AVERAGE(*argument1, argument2,...*)	Average of listed arguments
CEILING(*number,significance*)	Number rounded to nearest integer
CELL(*info_type,reference*)	Information about the upper-left cell in a reference
CHAR(*ASCII-code*)	Character matching ASCII code
CHOOSE(*index_number,value1, value2,...*)	A value from a list of value arguments
CLEAN(*text*)	*text* with all nonprintable characters removed
CODE(*text*)	ASCII code for first character in a text string
COLUMN(*range*)	Column numbers in a range
COLUMNS(*array*)	Number of columns in the array
COMBIN(*number,number_chosen*)	*Number* of combinations for number of chosen objects
CONCATENATE(*text1,text2,...*)	Combine up to 30 text items into a single text item
COS(*x*)	Cosine of *x*
COSH(*x*)	Hyperbolic cosine of *x*

Function	Returns
COUNT(*value1*,[*value2*],...)	Number of cells containing up to 30 numbers
COUNTA(*value1*,[*value2*],...)	Number of values in a list of up to 30 arguments
COUNTBLANK(*range*)	Number of blank cells in a *range*
COUNTIF(*range*,*criteria*)	Number of non-blank cells in a *range*
COUPDAYBS(*settlement*, *maturity*,*frequency*,[*basis*])	Number of days between start of coupon period and settlement date
COUPDAYS(*settlement*,*maturity*, *frequency*,[*basis*])	Number of days in the coupon period that contains the settlement date
COUPDAYSNC(*settlement*, *maturity*,*frequency*,[*basis*])	Number of days between the next coupon date and the settlement date
COUPNCD(*settlement*,*maturity*, *frequency*,[*basis*])	Date of the next coupon after the settlement date
COUPNUM(*settlement*,*maturity*, *frequency*,[*basis*])	Number of coupons payable from settlement to maturity
COUPPCD(*settlement*,*maturity*, *frequency*,[*basis*])	Last coupon date before the settlement date
CUMIPMT(*rate*,*nper*,*pv*, *start_period*,*end_period*,*type*)	Cumulative interest paid between *start_period* and *end_period*
CUMPRINC(*rate*,*nper*,*pv*, *start_period*,*end_period*,*type*)	Cumulative principal paid between *start_period* and *end_period*
DATE(*year*,*month*,*day*)	Date serial number

Function	Returns
DATEVALUE(*date_text*)	Date serial number for an actual date
DAVERAGE(*database, field,criteria*)	Average values for matching database records
DAY(*serial_number*)	Day number
DAYS360(*start_date,end_date,* [*method*])	Number of days between *start_date* and *end_date*
DB(*cost,salvage,life,period,* [*month*])	Depreciation using the fixed-declining balance method
DCOUNT(*database,* [*field*], *criteria*)	Number of cells with numbers in [*field*], or number of matching database records if no [*field*] is designated
DCOUNTA(*database,* [*field*],*criteria*)	Number of nonblank cells in *field*
DDB(*cost,salvage,life,* [*period*],[*factor*])	Depreciation using the double-declining balance method
DGET(*database,field,criteria*)	Single field that matches criteria
DISC(*settlement,maturity,pr, redemption,[basis]*)	Discount rate for a security
DMAX(*database,field,criteria*)	Largest number in field of records that match criteria
DMIN(*database,field,criteria*)	Smallest number in field of records that match criteria
DOLLAR(*number,[decimals]*)	*number* converted to text, rounded to specified decimals

Function	Returns
DOLLARDE(*fractional_dollar, fraction*)	Fractional dollar value as a decimal dollar value
DOLLARFR(*decimal_dollar, fraction*)	Decimal dollar value as a fractional dollar value
DPRODUCT(*database,field, criteria*)	Product of the *criteria* values found in *field*
DSTDEV(*database,field,criteria*)	Sample standard deviation for the field
DSTDEVP(*database,field,criteria*)	Population standard deviation for the field
DSUM(*database,field,criteria*)	Sum of the numbers in the field
DURATION(*settlement,maturity, coupon,yld,frequency,*[*basis*])	Annual Macauley duration for a security
DVAR(*database,field,criteria*)	Estimated variance
DVARP(*database,field,criteria*)	Population variance of all values in *field*
EDATE(*start_date,months*)	Date serial number for date indicated by number of *months* after *start_date*
EFFECT(*nominal_rate,npery*)	Effective annual interest rate
EOMONTH(*start_date,months*)	Serial number of the last day of the month occurring *months* after *start_date*
ERROR.TYPE(*error_val*)	Number representing type of error
EVEN(*x*)	Number rounded up to nearest even integer
EXACT(*text1,text2*)	TRUE if *text1* and *text2* match, FALSE if they don't match

Function	Returns
EXP(*x*)	*e* raised to the power of *x*
FACT(*x*)	Factorial of *x*
FACTDOUBLE(*x*)	Double factorial of *x*
FALSE()	Logical FALSE value
FASTMATCH(*lookup_value*, *lookup_array*,[*match_type*])	First number in the *lookup_array*
FIND(*find_text*,*within_text*, [*start_at_num*])	Position where found character appears
FIXED(*number*,[*decimals*], [*no_comma*])	*number* as text with fixed number of decimal places
FLOOR(*number*,*multiple_value*)	*number* rounded down to nearest *multiple_value*
FV(*rate*,*num_pmts*,*pmt*, [*pres_val*],[*type*])	Future value of an investment
FVSCHEDULE(*principle*, *schedule*)	Future value of *principle* based on *schedule* of compound interest rates
GCD(*number1*,[*number2*],...)	Greatest common divisor
HLOOKUP(*lookup_value*,*range*, *row_num*)	Value from top row of range
HOUR(*serial_num*)	Hour defined by serial number
IF(*logic_text*,*value_if_true*, *value_if_false*)	One value if true, another value if false
INDEX(*range*,[*row_num*], [*column_num*],[*area_num*]) or (*array*,[*row_num*],[*column_num*])	Value in specified row and column from a range or an array
INDIRECT(*ref_text*,[*a1*])	Reference indicated by text type (*a1*)
INFO(*type*)	Information about the operating environment

Function	Returns
INT(*x*)	*x* rounded down to nearest integer
INTRATE(*settlement,maturity, investment,redemption,* [*basis*])	Interest rate for fully invested security
IPMT(*rate,per,nper,pv,* [*fv*],[*type*])	Interest payment for a loan over a specified period
IRR(*values,*[*guess*])	Internal rate of return
ISBLANK(*x*)	TRUE if *x* is an empty cell
ISERR(*x*)	TRUE if *x* has an error value except #N/A
ISERROR(*x*)	TRUE if *x* has any error value
ISEVEN(*x*)	TRUE if *x* is even
ISLOGICAL(*x*)	TRUE if *x* is logical
ISNA(*x*)	TRUE if *x* is an #N/A value
ISNONTEXT(*x*)	TRUE if *x* is not text
ISNUMBER(*x*)	TRUE if *x* is a number
ISODD(*x*)	TRUE if *x* is an odd number
ISREF(*x*)	TRUE if *x* is a reference
ISTEXT(*x*)	TRUE if *x* contains or is text
LCM(*x*)	Least common multiple
LEFT(*text,*[*num_chars*])	Leftmost character(s) in a text string
LEN(*text*)	Number of characters in the text string
LN(*x*)	Natural logarithm of *x*
LOG(*x,*[*base*])	Logarithm of a number to a specified base

Function	Returns
LOG10(*x*)	Base 10 logarithm of *x*
LOOKUP(*lookup_value, lookup_range,result_range*)	Closest value to the *lookup_value* in a range
LOOKUP(*lookup_value,array*)	Value matching the *lookup_value* in an *array*
LOWER(*text*)	Lowercase letters for uppercase letters
MATCH(*lookup_value, lookup_array,[match_type]*)	Relative position of data entry that matches the *lookup_value*
MAX(*number1,[number2],...*)	Largest value in the list
MDETERM(*array*)	Matrix determinant of *array*
MDURATION(*settlement, maturity,coupon,yld, frequency,[basis]*)	Macauley modified duration assuming par value of $100
MEDIAN(*number1,[number2],...*)	Median of the listed numbers
MID(*text,start_num,num_chars*)	Specified number of characters in a text string
MIN(*number1,[number2],...*)	Smallest number in a list
MINUTE(*serial_number*)	Minutes corresponding to a time serial number
MINVERSE(*array*)	Matrix inverse of *array*
MIRR(*values,finance_rate, reinvest_rate*)	Internal rate of return for cash and outflows financed at different rates
MMULT(*array1,array2*)	Matrix product of *array1* and *array2*
MOD(*x,y*)	Remainder (modulus) of *x* divided by *y*
MONTH(*serial_number*)	Month of the year

Function	Returns
MROUND (*x,multiple*)	Number *x* rounded to the specified *multiple*
MULTINOMIAL(*number1*, [*number2*],...)	Multinomial of a group of numbers
N(*x*)	The value *x* converted to its corresponding number
NA()	#N/A (no value is available)
NETWORKDAYS(*start_date*, *end_date*,[*holidays*])	Number of work days between start and end date
NOMINAL(*effective_rate,npery*)	Nominal annual interest rate over a number of periods
NOT(*x*)	Opposite of the logical evaluation of *x*
NOW()	Serial number of current date and time
NPER(*rate,pmt,pv,*[*fv*],[*type*])	Number of periods for an investment
NPV(*rate,value1,*[*value2*],...)	Net present value for series of cash flow values
ODD(*x*)	*x* rounded up to nearest odd integer
ODDFPRICE(*settlement, maturity,issue,first_coupon, rate,yld,redemption, frequency,*[*basis*])	Price per $100 face value of a security with an odd first period
ODDFYIELD(*settlement, issue,first_coupon,rate,pr, redemption,frequency,*[*basis*])	Yield of a security with an odd first period
ODDLPRICE(*settlement, maturity,last_coupon,rate, yld,redemption,frequency,* [*basis*])	Price per $100 face value of a security with an odd last period

Function	Returns
ODDLYIELD(*settlement, maturity,last_coupon,rate,pr, redemption,frequency,[basis]*)	Yield of a security with an odd last period
OFFSET(*reference,rows,cols, [height],[width]*)	Reference offset from the given *reference*
OR(*logical1,[logical2],...*)	TRUE unless all arguments evaluate to FALSE
PERCENTILE(*array,K*)	*K*th percentile from the array
PERCENTRANK(*array,x, [significance]*)	Percentage rank of *x* in the array
PERMUT(*number, number_chosen*)	Number of permutations of groups selected from *number* objects
PI()	π (3.141592265359)
PMT(*rate,nper,pv,[fv],[type]*)	Periodic payment for a loan
POWER(*number,x*)	*Number* calculated to the power of *x*
PPMT(*rate,per,nper,pv,[fv], [type]*)	Payment on the principle for a loan
PRICE(*settlement,maturity, rate,yld,redemption, frequency,[basis]*)	Price per $100 face value of an interest-bearing security
PRICEDISC(*settlement, maturity,discount, redemption,[basis]*)	Price per $100 face value of a discounted security
PRICEMAT(*settlement,maturity, issue,rate,yld,[basis]*)	Price per $100 face value of a security whose interest is paid upon maturation
PRODUCT(*number1, [number2],...*)	Product of all the included arguments

Function	Returns
PROPER(*text*)	Capitalized first letter in each word of text
PV(*rate,nper,pmt,*[*fv*],[*type*])	Present value of an investment
QUOTIENT(*numerator, denominator*)	Whole number of *denominator* divided into *numerator*
RADIANS(*angle_in_degrees*)	Degrees converted into radians
RAND()	Random number equal to or greater than 0 and less than 1
RANDBETWEEN(*bottom,top*)	Random number within the specified range
RANK(*number,ref,*[*order*])	Rank of *number* in a list of values
RATE(*nper,pmt,pv,*[*fv*], [*type*],[*guess*])	Interest rate for a loan
RECEIVED(*settlement,maturity, investment,discount,*[*basis*])	Amount received for a fully invested security at maturity
REPLACE(*old_text,start_num, num_chars,new_text*)	*New_text* within *old_text*
REPT(*text,number_times*)	Text repeated a specified number of times
RIGHT(*text,*[*num_characters*])	Right-most character(s) in a string of text
ROMAN(*number,*[*form*])	Converts Arabic *number* to desired *form* of Roman numeral
ROUND(*x,*[*num_digits*])	*x* rounded to specified number of digits

Function	Returns
ROUNDDOWN(*x*,[*num_digits*])	Rounds *x* down to specified number of digits
ROUNDUP(*x*,[*num_digits*])	Rounds *x* up to specified number of digits
ROW(*range*)	Row numbers in a specified range
ROWS(*range*)	Number of rows in a specified range
SEARCH(*find_text*,*within_text*, [*start_num*])	Position where the *find_text* data is found
SECOND(*serial_number*)	Seconds for the specified time serial number
SERIESSUM(*x*,*n*,*m*,*coefficients*)	Sum of a power series of *x*
SIGN(*x*)	1 if *x* is positive, 0 if zero, -1 if negative
SIN(*x*)	Sine of the angle *x*
SINH(*x*)	Hyperbolic sine of *x*
SLN(*cost*,*salvage*,*life*)	Straight-line depreciation for an asset
SMALL(*array*,*K*)	*K*th smallest value in the array
SQRT(*x*)	Positive square root of *x*
SQRTPI(*x*)	Square root of *x* multiplied by π
STDEV(*number1*,[*number2*],...)	Estimated standard deviation for a list of arguments
STDEVP(*number1*,[*number2*],...)	Population standard deviation for a list of arguments
SUBSTITUTE(*text*,*old_text*, *new_text*,[*instance_num*])	*new_text* substituted for *old_text* in the *text* string

Function	Returns
SUBTOTAL(*function_num,ref*)	Subtotal in a list
SUM(*number1,*[*number2*],...)	Sum of numbers contained in numbered arguments
SUMIF(*range,criteria,* [*sum_range*])	Totals cells according to criteria
SUMPRODUCT(*array1,array2,* [*array3*],...)	Sum of the products of the specified arrays
SUMSQ(*number1,*[*number2*],...)	Sum of the squares of the listed arguments
SUMX2MY2(*array_x,array_y*)	Sum of the difference of squares of values in two arrays
SUMX2PY2(*array_x,array_y*)	Sum of the sum of squares of values in two arrays
SUMXMY2(*array_x,array_y*)	Sum of squares of differences of values in two arrays
SYD(*cost,salvage,life,per*)	Depreciation for an asset over a specified period
T(*x*)	Text if *x* is, or refers to, text
TAN(*x*)	Tangent of *x*
TANH(*x*)	Hyperbolic tangent of *x*
TBILLEQ(*settlement,maturity, discount*)	Bond-equivalent yield for a Treasury bill
TBILLPRICE(*settlement, maturity,discount*)	Price per $100 face value for a Treasury bill
TBILLYIELD(*settlement, maturity,discount*)	Yield for a Treasury bill
TEXT(*x,format_text*)	Converts *x* to text in the specified number format
TIME(*hour,minute,second*)	Time serial number

Function	Returns
TIMEVALUE(*time_text*)	Time serial number for *time_text*
TODAY()	Time serial number for the current date
TRANSPOSE(*array*)	Transpose of the specified array
TRIM(*text*)	Specified text with all spaces removed except single space between words
TRIMMEAN(*array,percent*)	Mean of data points after a percentage of the data points are removed from the array
TRUE()	Logical TRUE value
TRUNC(*x,[num_digits]*)	*x* with all numbers to the right of the decimal point removed except for the specified *num_digits*
TYPE(*x*)	Type of value represented by *x*
UPPER(*text*)	Lowercase text converted to uppercase
VALUE(*text*)	*Text* converted to a number
VAR(*number1,[number2],...*)	Estimated variance of a population
VARP(*number1,[number2],...*)	Variance of a population
VDB(*cost,salvage,life, start_period,end_period, [factor],[no_switch]*)	Depreciation of an asset
VLOOKUP(*lookup_value, table_array,col_index_num, [range_lookup]*)	Value in the first column of the array

Function	Returns
WEEKDAY(*serial_number, return_type*)	Day of the week
WORKDAY(*start_date,days, holidays*)	Serial number date for day a specified number of days after the *start_date*
XIRR(*values,dates,[guess]*)	Internal rate of return for a schedule of cash flows
XNPV(*rate,values,dates*)	Net present value for a schedule of cash flows
YEAR(*serial_number*)	Year between 1900 and 2078
YEARFRAC(*start_date,end_date,* [*basis*])	Fraction of year representing number of whole days between *start_date* and *end_date*
YIELD(*settlement,maturity, rate,pr,redemption,frequency,* [*basis*])	Yield on a security that pays periodic interest
YIELDDISC(*settlement, maturity,pr,redemption,* [*basis*])	Yield for a discounted security
YIELDMAT(*settlement,maturity, issue,rate,pr,*[*basis*])	Yield of security that pays interest upon maturation

Index